DOWN TO DONINGTON

The story of the first

Jerry Bloom
Foreword by Don Airey

*This book is dedicated to the
memory of Cozy Powell.
A man whose company I was fortunate to
have enjoyed the year before his passing
and who in my mind was an as
larger-than-life rock 'n' roll character
as you could wish for.*

Jerry Bloom

DOWN TO DONINGTON

The story of the first

Jerry Bloom
Foreword by Don Airey

First published in 2017 under the title *Monsters of Rock Donington 1980*.
This revised, expanded edition published in 2025 by
Wymer Publishing Bedford, England
www.wymerpublishing.co.uk Tel: 01234 326691
Wymer Publishing is a trading name of Wymer (UK) Ltd

Copyright © 2025 Jerry Bloom / Wymer Publishing.

ISBN: 978-1-915246-86-8

The Author hereby asserts their rights to be identified
as the author of this work in accordance with sections
77 to 78 of the Copyright, Designs & Patents Act 1988.

All rights reserved. No part of this publication may be
reproduced or transmitted in any form or by any means,
electronic or mechanical, including photocopying, or any
information storage and retrieval system, without written
permission from the publisher.

This publication is sold subject to the condition that it shall not,
by way of trade or otherwise, be lent, re-sold, hired out or
otherwise circulated without the publishers' prior consent in any
form of binding or cover other than that in which it is published
and without a similar condition including this condition
being imposed on the subsequent purchaser.

eBook formatting by Lin White at Coinlea.

A catalogue record for this book is available from the British Library.

Typeset/Design by Andy Bishop / Tusseheia Creative
Cover design by Jerry Bloom / Tusseheia Creative

Contents

Foreword by Don Airey	7
Preface	11
1. You Didn't Come Just To See The Show	17
2. No Time To Lose	27
3. Danger Zone	39
4. In The Eyes Of The World	49
5. I Guess You Know What You Wanna See	59
6. Down To Colin	83
7. Broken Dreams In The Ground	89
8. I Saw You Standing Down By The Stage	97
Appendices	111
Set lists	111
Acknowledgements	119

Foreword

The first Donington Festival was not only a personal turning point in my life, but also in the life of British Heavy Rock. Up to that point if you wanted to play a festival the choice was limited to a few disorganised mud-strewn events out in the Boonies of Europe, or at home playing Reading which only booked Blues or Pop bands.

Rainbow were sitting round the lobby of the Holiday Inn, Newcastle bemoaning the fact there was nothing anymore to rival Woodstock or the California Jam, when Cozy Powell suggested we hold our own festival. "Let's book a racetrack!" As he had raced saloon cars at Donington and knew the owners, he gave them a call. The answer was an immediate "Yes," and within a few days we had got promoter Maurice Jones on board, who in turn quickly booked an impressive line-up of like-minded musicians for August a few months hence.

The soundcheck the day before the gig was in many ways as memorable as the event itself. Cozy fulfilled his lifelong ambition of creating the loudest explosion ever heard on a rock stage, during the drum solo, in the process blowing every cone out of the PA (a spectacular albeit costly sight).

It was raining heavily and Maurice Jones in a thoughtful touch kitted all the bands out with Wellington Boots (I still have mine). Judas Priest arrived to check their gear looking mean and moody in black leather (and wellies) and blew us all away with the precision and impact of their priestly riffs. Ritchie Blackmore stroking his chin, commented "It doesn't do to get too complacent in this business."

Come the day, the rain abated, though leaving plenty of obligatory mud, which in no way dampened the enthusiasm of a crowd 50,000 strong who were treated to a succession of brilliant sets— openers Touch, April Wine, Saxon, the Scorpions, Riot and of course Priest all stepping up to the plate.

Rainbow playing the headline spot in the wake of the success of *Down To Earth*, went on stage in a shower of pyro. Ritchie played the closest to Hendrix I ever heard anyone manage, even though he omitted the promised solo atop the PA stack after my wife, unaware of his plans, told him of a dream she'd had a few days previously in which he'd tumbled off.

During the keyboard solo, doing my Close-Encounters-Spaceship-Landing bit, an airliner heading for the adjacent airport swooped over the crowd with perfect timing, as though we had paid the pilot to do just that. Ozzy Osbourne who was watching in the wings with Gary Moore, later told me Graham Bonnet's performance was the greatest he had ever seen by a vocalist.

Rainbow walked off stage in triumph, and the best band I was ever in, playing arguably the greatest fest ever held on British soil promptly split up—Cozy, for reasons unknown, went off to join MSG, Graham left because Cozy had gone.

Nothing was ever quite the same again for me and though I must have played 200 festivals since, none has captured the magic of the day when heavy metal emerged from the underground into the mainstream. So, sit back, relax and enjoy the story and pictures from a landmark event—Monsters of Rock, Castle Donington, August 16th, 1980. It was a Brahma!

Don Airey, Cambridgeshire

Preface

Outdoor music festivals have been a staple of the yearly calendar almost from the outset of rock 'n' roll, although the first such events actually catered for different genres.

One of the earliest British festivals was the Beaulieu Jazz Festival, started in 1956 by Lord Montagu of Beaulieu and held in the grounds of the Beaulieu estate in the New Forest. It catered for traditional and modern jazz, but it soon expanded to include both pop and jazz.

In the States the Newport Folk Festival had started two years earlier in 1954 and back in Britain the National Jazz Festival was created by Harold Pendleton, the founder of the prestigious Marquee Club in Soho, with the first event being staged in 1961.

By 1964 it was renamed the National Jazz & Blues Festival. In 1971 when it moved to a new site in Reading it was again renamed as the National Jazz, Blues & Rock Festival, catering for the expanding rock market at the expense of the decline in popularity in jazz—eventually it was simply referred to as the Reading Festival.

In 1968 the first Isle of Wight concert was staged to an audience of approximately 10,000 and essentially aimed at progressive and underground rock with headliners Jefferson Airplane and a support cast that included Tyrannosaurus Rex, Aynsley Dunbar's Retaliation and The Pretty Things.

The following year the two-day event played host to around 150,000, largely drawn to it by Bob Dylan and The Who.

By its third year it had expanded into a five-day festival and included an even grander array of artists including Jimi Hendrix, Miles Davis, Jethro Tull, Ten Years After, Chicago, The Doors, The Who, Emerson, Lake & Palmer, The Moody Blues and Free.

An estimate of around 600,000 attended over the week but such a large gathering met with much disapproval from the local council and residents.

It led in 1971 to Parliament passing the "Isle of Wight Act" preventing gatherings of more than 5,000 people on the island without a special license which put paid to the festival until it was reactivated in 2002.

Meanwhile the Reading Festival went from strength to strength and by the late seventies it was largely catering for a mix of traditional rock and New Wave and punk acts.

Likewise, the Knebworth festivals of the seventies often had an array of different styles of acts. Although no show was put on in '77, in 1978,

there were two Knebworths—the first in June with a mixture of bands, from headliners Genesis to the likes of Tom Petty and the Heartbreakers, to Devo. The second one held in September was equally as eclectic with The Tubes, Frank Zappa, The Boomtown Rats and Peter Gabriel.

Even the 1979 Knebworth, which saw the return of Led Zeppelin who performed over two consecutive weekends, had a real cross-section of other acts on the bill including Southside Johnny and The Asbury Jukes, Fairport Convention and Chas and Dave!

When in 1980 the first Donington Festival was staged it was the first major event that focused on one genre. Such an approach had up to then been fairly alien to promoters. Whether or not it was a reflection of the changing times is difficult to be certain.

Of the festivals I attended in the late seventies and some in the early eighties the audiences were obviously largely made up of fans of the headliners and some sections of the crowds were quite hostile to different genres.

Such a narrow perspective of music isn't one I personally subscribe to but having witnessed such a response at first hand; the likelihood of such things happening with all the acts in a similar style was certainly diminished.

Perhaps a decade on from the likes of Isle of Wight, more and more music fans were becoming less open minded? Pure speculation of course, but certainly when the Monsters of Rock Festival was conceived its remit was to stick to heavy rock bands—no Chas and Dave or Fairport Convention was going to be gracing the stage at Donington Park!

As it turned out, it proved to be a winning formula. Although the first one, which this book celebrates did not attract anywhere near the same size of crowds as those that followed did, as the inaugural one it will always be held with great affection.

An article published in *The Observer* in 2015 entitled "twelve moments that made the modern music festival" chose Donington 1980 as one of its twelve. Considering by then it had six decades of music and events to factor in, it shows what an impact that gig in the middle of a muddy racetrack on a sunny August day in 1980 has had: One that clearly still resonates nearly forty years on.

Much of this text was originally written to accompany the now out of print *Monsters of Rock Donington 1980*, hardback photographic book published in 2017.

For this book I have revisited the story and added to it with additional research. Much of which has proved to be very enlightening. It reveals that it was touch and go whether or not the event was going to get cancelled with just a couple of weeks to go before the big day.

SPECIAL MEETING ON ROCK FESTIVAL

Leicestershire County Council's Planning Sub-committee is meeting today to decide what action to take, if any, over the proposed rock festival at Castle Donington Race Circuit on August 16.

Views sought on future of rock concert

You Didn't Come Just To See The Show

Credit for the Monsters of Rock Festival becoming a heavy rock legacy falls squarely on the shoulders of two men—Paul Loasby and Maurice Jones, although it all came about rather quickly.

In October 1979 Harvey Goldsmith along with fellow promoter Alec Leslie set up Umbrella Productions. The same month Loasby who had been working for Goldsmith jointly promoted The Stranglers UK tour with Britain's biggest promoter and in doing so started to establish his own name at the same time.

Unfortunately, some mentions of his name made the press for the wrong reasons.

On 31st October '79 The Stranglers tour was coming to its conclusion. Following a gig at the Top Rank in Cardiff, along with Stranglers' front man Hugh Cornwell, Loasby departed Wales in a hire-car for an overnight drive to the capital, where the tour was to conclude at the Rainbow Theatre.

At 3:00am, 1st November, with the car having just pulled off the A4, when they reached Hammersmith Broadway, the pair were confronted with a police stop-check.

The car was full of drugs and both men were charged with possession. Fortunately, the gig at the Rainbow went ahead that evening, as did the rest of the touring plans in mainland Europe and Japan that rounded off the year whilst they awaited their court hearing.

Cornwell and Loasby started the New Year in the dock at Knightsbridge Crown Court. Loasby was feeling confident that they would get let off with a caution, but nothing could have been further from the truth.

Cornwell was sentenced to eight weeks in prison and fined £300 after admitting to five charges of possessing drugs, including cannabis, heroin and cocaine. Loasby admitted possessing cocaine and received a fourteen-day sentence.

In summing up, magistrate Eric Crowther said, "You are two intellectual men of mature ages who have a great influence on the lifestyle of teenagers and who should not cause damage to the morals and physical well-being of those who admire you. Both of you have a university education which makes your involvement in the drug scene all the more contemptible. You have deliberately chosen to flaunt the law."

For the Stranglers it put paid to their immediate

activities, but soon after this unfortunate interlude, Loasby was back up and running.

In early 1980 the new look Rainbow announced its first UK tour since 1977. In 1978 they concentrated on the American market but by December lead singer Ronnie James Dio had quit and Rainbow was in a state of flux while they looked for a replacement.

In fact, with Ritchie Blackmore also dispensing with the services of Bob Daisley and David Stone, at this point Rainbow consisted of just Blackmore and drummer Cozy Powell!

Through Powell, Don Airey was soon brought in on keyboards. Whilst Blackmore also drafted in his former Deep Purple colleague Roger Glover to produce the next album, but the band spent many weeks floundering before eventually hitting on former Marbles vocalist Graham Bonnet. With Glover also slotting in on bass the band was back up to full strength and the album *Down To Earth* was eventually recorded in early '79 and was released in August of that year.

Blackmore was still driven by his desire to crack the American market, but whilst the new, more commercial sounding Rainbow had an instant UK hit with 'Since You Been Gone' and the album climbed up the British charts, Rainbow spent the rest of 1979 once again touring the States.

Therefore, the band's first UK tour for two and a half years was met with much anticipation for the growing fan base. Paul Loasby was the promoter whose name was on the tickets, but as stated, "for Umbrella Productions."

Rainbow had begun the tour in Europe before the UK leg, which began on 19th February with two nights at Newcastle City Hall. Many of the gigs were bigger venues than Rainbow had previously played and the dates in February and March proved to be the band's most successful UK tour at the time, with Loasby in the thick of it.

This tour also saw a variety of different support bands including the relatively new band Saxon as guests for two of the shows at the New Bingley Hall in Stafford and Deeside Leisure Centre.

For Saxon's Graham Oliver it was the chance to rub shoulders with a band he had seen a few years earlier: "In 1976, I saw Rainbow in Manchester. At that time, Steve Dawson and I had just invited Biff Byford to sing with our band SOB. He brought in Paul Quinn to the band too, and later SOB was changed to Son Of A Bitch for a couple of years, then to Saxon."

Through the mists of time Oliver's memory has got the better of him as his recollection is that these were the first dates of the tour, but Rainbow had already played Newcastle and Edinburgh.

They were simply the first dates with Saxon, as Samson had opened at the previous shows.

"We were recording *Wheels of Steel*... Next thing we were offered a tour with Rainbow, and the first gig was at Deeside Leisure Centre. At this point, Saxon had just done the Motörhead tour to great reviews. The first gig went great, but we had no contact with the band. The second gig was Bingley Hall Stafford. Ritchie had his own dressing room next to ours. We found a hole in the wall and spied on him getting ready for his show. We did our set and killed 'em. When we returned to the dressing room, Ritchie had a ritual of music played just before he went on stage playing: Jethro Tull, Hendrix, and the film music from the movie *Chariots of Fire*. Then, bam—they hit the stage! Rainbow were fantastic, and Cozy's solo was awesome (Steve and I had played a gig in '74 and met Cozy before, but he did not remember). We met the band, minus Ritchie, after the show. But the day after, we got canned from the tour. Samson replaced us as I recall."

Samson did indeed support at some shows, including the gig that followed Deeside—Wembley Arena on 29th February—the notorious gig where Blackmore chose not to do an encore, which sparked a mini riot and significant damage to the venue.

But for the second of two nights in London not only did Blackmore behave himself with a lengthier show, including a full guitar smashing encore, but The Troggs were on the bill for that gig.

Later, on that same tour Blackmore agreed to be interviewed by a few fans backstage at Brighton for *Sounds* magazine. One question that cropped up was about some of the new bands such as Iron Maiden, Def Leppard and particularly Saxon as some of the fans had been hoping to see them as the support act.

Blackmore gave his reasons as to why they were taken off the tour: "I spoke to some fans outside one of the gigs early on in the tour and they'd really enjoyed it, but I asked them if they had any criticisms. They said the group on with us that night they had seen with Ian Gillan. So, then I investigated a little more and decided that if that was the case then we should get another band. Samson are a really good group, like Saxon, but I think in seeing them again the fans were being cheated. That has nothing to do with how good or bad the band happens to be. Like somebody said that Saxon were too good for us and that's why they didn't do the rest of the tour, which wasn't true at all. That really pissed me off."

****

As Don Airey mentions in his foreword, it was during the tour that Cozy Powell suggested an open-air gig to top off their return to the UK. One thing led to another and before long Rainbow's management was in discussion with Loasby, who along with Maurice Jones, mapped out the plans for a one-day festival dedicated specifically for hard rock bands.

Born in the West Midlands town of Wednesbury, Maurice Jones began dabbling in the music business while serving his apprenticeship at John

Thompson's engineering works in Wolverhampton where he used a public phone box as his first office, managing an act called the 'N Betweens who later became Slade.

At the age of 19 he joined the Astra Agency in Wolverhampton as a booker and became heavily involved in Club Lafayette where he booked the likes of Led Zeppelin, Yes and John Mayall and the Bluesbreakers.

In 1977 he quit Astra to form his own business, Midland Concert Promotions (MCP), which — as the name suggests — saw him remain true to his roots, being located in Walsall.

Whilst Loasby was discussing the possibilities with Rainbow's manager Bruce Payne of topping off the UK tour with a big show in the summer, Maurice Jones happened to know Tom Wheatcroft, the owner of the Donington Park racetrack, located next to the village of Castle Donington in Leicestershire.

It seemed to be an ideal location. Although Donington Park was unfamiliar outside of motor racing as a major venue, its central location and excellent road access with the M1, A42 and A50 allowed for good transportation to the site from around the country. Additionally, the ground level sloped which allowed for a better viewing experience for the audience throughout the site.

It could also be claimed that as Loasby's vision was for a festival that focused on one specific genre; given that heavy rock appeared to be particularly popular in the industrial heartlands of England's Midlands and North, this was another good reason for choosing it.

With one-day festival tickets invariably at the time being around double the price of an indoor gig, getting several bands for double the price was promoting better value for money. Also, by using a midlands location, it was certainly less of a distance for many rock devotees to travel than the annual Reading Festival.

As always Reading had a cross-section of bands but in 1980 the three-day festival included many heavy acts. When the Reading line-up was announced there were plenty of bands to cater for heavy rock fans. On the Friday the bill included Krokus, Praying Mantis and Gillan. Saturday saw headliners UFO along with Iron Maiden and Samson and on the Sunday Whitesnake, Def Leppard and Ozzy Osbourne's Blizzard of Oz. Although the latter band ended up not playing and seventies glam rockers Slade were brought in at short notice, there was still an impressive number of bands but a full weekend ticket cost £12.50.

Tickets for Donington were £7.50 in advance or £8.50 on the day but despite the longer distance to travel to Reading for rock fans from the north; hosting a new rock festival the week before the established three-day festival was a bold move for Loasby and Jones. Sure, some fans would surely lap up the opportunity to do both, but for those on tighter budgets, shelling out for tickets for two events so closely together was bound to have some impact on both festivals.

Open-air pop festival may be banned

Rock fans are reassured over refunds

No Time To Lose

Donington was naturally built around Rainbow. Along with the successful UK tour they had also achieved another equally successful chart hit with 'All Night Long' and had appeared on *Top of The Pops* with both hit singles.

The suave look of lead singer Graham Bonnet was cutting home with the new legion of fans that national TV exposure had given them and it certainly increased the band's profile no end.

The next step was to put together a supporting cast that would add to the attraction. When it was first announced in the press both Sammy Hagar and Black Sabbath were talked of as possible inclusions. Sabbath would have been interesting given that they were then fronted by Ronnie James Dio who had left Rainbow for his "heaven and hell." There were even press adverts that mentioned Sammy Hagar although nothing came of it.

In the end, with no Sabbath but the festival being based in the Midlands it seemed to make

perfect sense that Judas Priest was selected as the main support act. Hailing from Birmingham, the birthplace of Black Sabbath amongst others, Judas Priest had already notched up several successful albums and by the time of Donington, their previous four albums were all big sellers.

The success really kicked off with 1977's *Sin After Sin* which had been produced by Roger Glover of all people. Their acquaintance was to be renewed on the Donington racetrack in Leicestershire.

1980 was a busy year for Priest and following British and German tours in March and April, they spent most of the summer touring the States, ensuring they were more than road-ready by the time of Donington.

Priest frontman Rob Halford said later of this inaugural event, "We were very aware that it was the first festival of its type in the UK and was a major event in that respect. All the festivals that had happened in the UK before had, had a cross-section of bands, so this was the first to go with specifically one type of music. Our reaction when we first heard about it was that we'd like to give it a crack."

The next band on the bill—Scorpions—had a history that stretched back further than Blackmore's previous band Deep Purple. The German group had been initially formed in 1965 by Rudolf Schenker but there had been many years of hard graft before they even managed to release their first record in 1972. It was still many more years before Scorpions really started to make inroads into the UK market.

The release of *Lovedrive* in 1979 was their first album to break into the UK charts. By the time of Donington, Scorpions was on the ascendancy and perfectly suited for the first Monsters of Rock festival.

It's safe to say that the impetus for the festival was partly driven by the emergence of many new heavy bands over the previous couple of years or so. This sudden surge coined the phrase The New Wave of British Heavy Metal, credited to *Sounds* journalist Geoff Barton in May 1979.

With the Punk bubble having seemingly exploded, lots of new bands were emerging that took their influences from the heavier bands that had dominated the scene in the early years of the seventies.

However, whether by design or not, Loasby's line-up for the festival did not exactly reflect this growing movement. Instead, as well as the German Scorpions, it was a very international bill. Next up was Canadian outfit April Wine. Like Judas Priest their career stretched back to 1969, albeit in Halifax, the capital of the wilderness state of Nova Scotia.

Whilst Scorpions were one of a handful of German bands that had made an impact in Britain, likewise not too many Canadian bands had done so. The first that springs to mind is Steppenwolf and ironically the lyrics of their biggest hit 'Born

To Be Wild' introduced the term "heavy metal" to rock music.

Soon picked up on by American journalists, Brits were less enthusiastic in using the terminology and in fact some British bands, chief amongst them being Led Zeppelin were keen to disassociate themselves from such tags.

Other Canadian bands that slip off the tongue are Bachman Turner Overdrive and Rush, but the average UK rock fan would struggle to name too many. April Wine certainly was not one that resonated with great swathes of British rock fans but back home in their native Canada they had achieved a great level of success.

Like Scorpions, 1979 had seen the start of greater popularity outside their homeland. The band's seventh album, *First Glance* was their first Gold record outside of Canada and was very successful in the States.

In the UK their albums had only started to get released from 1976 onwards but had made little impact. Following gigs in the States in January, April Wine toured Europe the following month.

A gig at Reading University in February was recorded for the BBC's *Rock Goes To College* show. The following month some German and Dutch dates were followed by a handful of UK shows including Hammersmith Odeon with support from Angel Witch and Sledgehammer.

Clearly the band's label, Capitol Records wanted to capitalise on those shows and saw that the exposure the Donington festival would give them could only help their profile in the UK. In between the indoor dates and Donington the band returned to North America for further dates in Canada and USA.

The only band on the bill that fitted Barton's "New Wave of British Heavy Metal" moniker was Saxon. These fresh-faced lads from Barnsley had released their debut album in '79 but it was the follow up, *Wheels Of Steel*, released three months before the Monsters of Rock gig, that really started to get them noticed.

The title track was also released as a single and gave them somewhat unexpected exposure on *Top of The Pops*, as Byford recalled years later in an interview with Joe Geesin: "The first time was for *Wheels Of Steel*. We got this phone call: it had gone into the charts at No. 31 or something and we needed to play *Top of The Pops*. We did it a few days before, in a studio on our own. It was bizarre, really: lip-syncing, no audience. We wanted to play live but couldn't get all our gear in. A bit scary to do, but we did it in fifteen minutes."

Completing the bill was two American bands, Riot and Touch. Riot was formed in 1975 in New York City when Kon-Tiki guitarist Mark Reale and drummer Peter Bitelli recruited bassist Phil Feit and vocalist Guy Speranza. The soon added Steve Costello on keyboards followed by second guitarist Louie Kouvaris and replaced Feit with Jimmy Iommi during the making of their debut album,

Rock City with both bass players recording on it. After a promising start and support slots with AC/DC and Molly Hatchet, the band were unable to maintain momentum and were on the verge of breaking up for good by 1979.

Fortunately, they had a lucky break on the other side of the Atlantic. In that year influential British DJ Neal Kaye and a champion of the New Wave of British Heavy Metal, brought Riot to the attention of British rock fans who bought imported copies of *Rock City* and gave new life to the band.

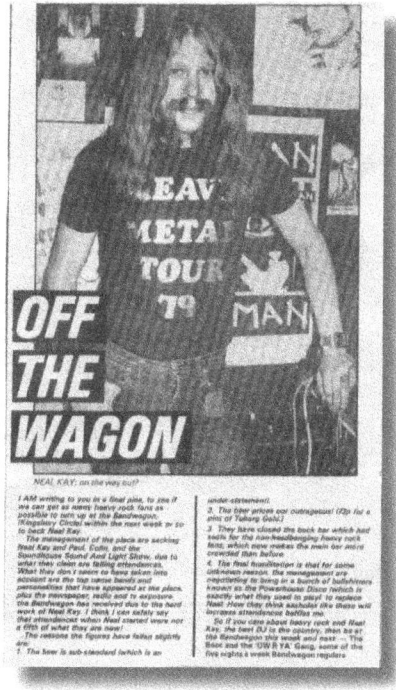

Touch was also from New York City having formed in 1978. Mark Mangold (songwriter and keyboards), Glen Kithcart (drums), and Craig Brooks (guitars) had all previously been in the band American Tears (releasing three albums on Columbia Records). The line-up was completed by bassist Doug Howard. Thames Talent, Rainbow's management had taken Touch under its wing, which explains their addition to the bill.

In doing so they became the first band to grace the Monsters of Rock Festival although they were not the first part of the show to take the stage. That honour went to the aforementioned DJ Neal Kay, whose name was spelt incorrectly on the advertising posters and gig programme. As torch holder for all things heavy Kay was given the job of compère for the day.

Kay had always been a DJ. He started out in his local youth club in the mid-sixties and by the end of the decade was a well-established London-based nightclub DJ, working fully six nights a week. In 1969 he went to West Berlin with his future first wife, a dancer, to guest DJ in two clubs a night from dusk until dawn. His main club in Berlin was the Playboy Club. He also guested from time to time with the British Army.

In the period between 1975 and 1980, he managed a rock club called The Bandwagon Heavy Metal Soundhouse, originally resident in the backroom of the Prince of Wales public house in Kingsbury, North London; it was simply referred

to as 'The Bandwagon.'

With help from the music papers of the day, *Sounds* and *Melody Maker*, he went on to establish this venue as the place for new upcoming bands and like-minded fans. Kay had one of the biggest club sound systems ever seen at the time — an 8000 watt PA that he used to play his large collection of classic rock vinyl on. The PA was so loud that the mixing desk was flown on chains, suspended from the roof to help avoid feedback from the record decks.

With such credentials, Kay was the perfect choice to compère this inaugural heavy rock fest although despite his experience as a DJ, he later admitted to being anxious about the whole event: "I compèred the gig. I was nervous—I've never faced a crowd that big before. But when I walked out on that huge stage, the first ten rows were all Soundhouse members."

Over 50,000 fans expected

ROCK CONCERT PLAN WORRIES VILLAGERS

Over 50,000 rock music fans are expected to attend a concert at Donington Park in August — and villagers of Castle Donington are worried it might bring trouble.

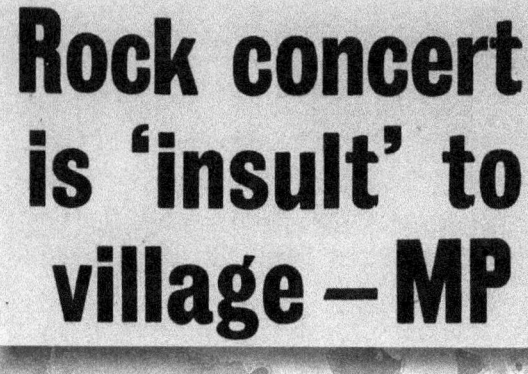

Rock concert is 'insult' to village – MP

Danger Zone

When the gig was announced there were the usual concerns from local residents whenever any large outdoor concert occurs.

One of the more illogical concerns stemmed around the image of the typical rock fan. Particularly the association with motor bikes.

Given that locals were used to race meetings for both cars and bikes, it seemed odd that there should be concerns about a percentage of the stereotypical biker.

Bill Clark, landlord of the Moira Arms pub in the village of Castle Donington said, "I think it is appalling this should be dropped out of the blue on the community. The Park management ought to consider the views of the people living in the vicinity before they decide to disrupt the life of the village."

Ironically Clark confessed to being a motorcyclist himself, but he was adamant that a small percentage of bikers cause trouble. As far as he was concerned, as long as they were contained within the Park and didn't venture into the village, he would be content.

Another landlord, Reg Saunders of the Donington Arms, had been forced to call the police on one occasion the previous year when there was a major motor-cycle meeting at the Park and as a result had banned bikers from his pub.

"It is unfortunate for the local lads," as Saunders told *The Stapleford and Sandiacre News*. "But they know if they want a drink here, they have to take their leathers off."

Presumably Saunders was of the view that the clothing determined behaviour!

Castle Donington Parish Council met on Thursday 26th June. One member Joyce Liddle said, "I don't think this will be very well received because whenever there are a lot of people on motorcycles in the village there tends to be a disturbance."

The councillors appeared to be particularly peeved because the first they learnt of it was through the press.

Clerk of the Council Dennis Bradburn thought that it would cost ratepayers a lot of money for extra policing.

A spokesman for Donington Park tried to assure the villagers that their concerns would be met. "The Harvey Goldsmith Organisation have a very good reputation and we were very receptive to their proposals. There will be a number of safeguards which are the subject of a contract being drawn up at the moment. The event will be held in the centre of the circuit so that it is enclosed within the perimeter." His words clearly designed to pacify any dissenters.

"It is no good having an event which is unsatisfactory. We have had too much experience of things that have been unsatisfactory and we consider the feelings of the residents and operate with that in mind."

For Maurice Jones and his Midlands Concert Promotions, although they arranged about three-hundred concerts a year, the Monsters of Rock event was the biggest they had ever promoted.

Jones let it be known that the music wouldn't be as loud as the cars that normally race around the track and assured concert goers that there would be extra toilet facilities and more than adequate catering.

Furthermore, Jones predicted that if the concert was a success, it could become an annual event.

By July the full line-up was in place, but the concert was potentially on the verge of being banned. Residents of Castle Donington were concerned about potential disturbances from noise and violence and demanded the event be cancelled.

Leicester County Council's chief planner Maurice Pettifor threw a spanner in the works when he said that no music was allowed to be relayed on any days other than pre-race days and race days.

Loughborough's MP Stephen Dorrell got involved and expressed his concerns with the legality of the event proposal. He asked the planning department to keep him informed of developments.

Pettifor told the *Leicester Mercury* that the racetrack was reminded of the conditions and Peter Gaydon the circuit's managing director confirmed that they were aware of them.

Gaydon appeared at ease with the situation, merely reiterating that outside promoters were asking to rent Donington Park and that the idea of a festival was still being investigated by everyone concerned.

Dorrell in a letter to Leicestershire's planning department was adamant that it was too late for any application to vary the planning permission. "It cannot be over-emphasised that any attempt to speed up the normal planning process in this 'special case' would bring the whole planning system into disrepute."

Meanwhile the promoters and bands carried on with planning. Rainbow's publicist Jennie Halsall said, "Rainbow swore that they would never take part in a festival such as this, but they have now agreed. They are doing it purely for the fans and the money they receive for appearing is being ploughed straight back into the show."

Like all publicists, Halsall's job was to

accentuate positives. Rainbow's early years had largely been financed by Blackmore's wealth, previously generated with Deep Purple. Now with a more commercial sound and hit singles, Rainbow was moving out of the red and into the black. In that context Halsall's comment could be taken with a pinch of salt.

Meanwhile Paul Loasby had apparently promised a "mystery" act. Writing in his *Pop* column for the *Leicester Mercury*, Dave Watson said, "which I understand may be Blue Öyster Cult." Needless to say, it came to nothing, although Blue Öyster Cult did appear at the event the following year.

Watson's column also mentioned of plans in place to film the festival for a television special.

By 18th July 15,000 tickets had been sold, pulling in £112,500. Many fans were anxious that if the concert was pulled that they wouldn't get a refund. After all, the terms of sale printed on the back of the tickets clearly stated: "Tickets cannot be exchanged or monies refunded for any reason whatsoever, including cancellation of the concert."

Maurice Jones was quick to say that the clause should have been modified before printing. "If the show is cancelled, we will refund the face value of the tickets, but people won't be allowed to claim for damages."

Maurice Pettifor was still of the view that "this concert would be contrary to planning agreements we have with Donington Park concerning the transmission of music."

Peter Gaydon counteracted this by saying that their legal advisors had examined the council's planning rules and given the go ahead.

"They are not using our speaker system, so the condition does not affect it," said Gaydon.

Pettifor informed that a decision would be made the following week on whether or not to take action. "We received the letter from their legal advisors today. This will be considered," he said.

Pettifor made it be known that a special meeting of the planning sub-committee could be called if an injunction was felt necessary.

Come 22nd July Maurice Pettifor again reasserted that having looked at the legal position the Council had come to the conclusion that because of the planning permission granted for the circuit, additional permission for the festival would have to be obtained.

Gaydon's solicitors were still taking the contrary view. "We are waiting for that verbal information to be sent to us in writing," said Pettifor. "In the meantime, we have arranged a special meeting of the Planning Sub-committee to consider what we are going to do or not do."

Pettifor added that there had been "fiery" representations from local people about the proposed festival.

Gaydon held his ground and said, "He was delighted the circuit was to host the fantastic event and he hoped Donington would become a top venue for Paul Loasby and Woolteare Ltd in the future."

On 25th July the *Leicester Mercury* reported that the concert was going ahead. Leicestershire County Council's planning committee decided not to oppose the festival but by no means did they support it. The planners decided after long debate not to seek an injunction. Several members felt they could find themselves saddled with heavy compensation if their case went wrong. But they were determined to monitor the festival closely to ensure that if necessary similar future events can be brought more within the planning legislation.

Meanwhile, the week before the concert, Don Airey spoke to Paul Cole of the *Black Country Evening Mail*. Cole suggested that few bands would relish the near-suicidal prospect of following Judas Priest on stage in their Midlands homeland. Rainbow just loved the idea.

Said Airey: "We weren't too sure that Rob Halford and the lads in Judas Priest would play support even though Roger Glover helped produce them at one stage. We wanted very much to get them because they provide a great contrast to our own music and they'll make us work hard. The Priest sound sets our own off nicely. Added to that is the fact that they're probably the biggest band in the Midlands right now and a lot of their fans will get a good chance to see them in action at home."

Airey explained that "We sent out special invitations to Judas Priest, Scorpions and Saxon to join us on the bill and the promoters sorted out the rest."

He added, "We never wanted to do an open-air festival before because we had all had such bad experiences with them in our other bands. But things are different now and we chose the Midlands because it's a heavy rock stronghold."

Three days before the concert it was still filling column inches concerning the ongoing divide between the authorities and the festival organisers.

Leicestershire County Council was being urged by Loughborough's MP Stephen Dorrell to seek a limitation of planning permission to exclude future rock festivals at the race circuit. Dorrell promised to press the case in Whitehall.

In a letter to Mr. R Angrave, chairman of the county's planning committee Dorrell said the relationship between Castle Donington and the racetrack was already strained and the decision of the council to allow a rock festival to go ahead had been seen as adding insult to injury.

In Dorrell's view, none of the explanations given for allowing the festival adequately answered the point that the original planning permission explicitly ruled out the playing of music over the public address system except on race days and pre-race practise days and that only a low-level short-throw speaker system could be used.

Dorrell said, "The impression has been allowed to gain ground and the instance of this rock festival can only substantially strengthen the impression, that the racetrack operators have repeatedly presented the authority with fait accompli situations which they have dared not interfere with."

With Peter Gaydon and the Donington Park legal team coming out on top, Gaydon said, "We have investigated thoroughly the regulations that govern all events at Donington and we have taken legal advice from the very highest levels. The results of those investigations show conclusively that Donington is perfectly entitled to hold such an event."

District Planning Officer Christopher North said, "At the end of the day the district council felt because the racetrack was designed for large crowds there were no highway causes or general planning reasons to prevent it being held."

Gaydon, Loasby, Jones et al had won the day. Now it was all systems go.

Rainbow... back in the open air!

TOP rock band Rainbow once vowed they would never perform at an open-air concert. But gentle persuasion has made them the headlining act at the monsters of Rock Festival at Castle Donington next month.

It will be Rainbow's second appearance in Leicestershire in five months - they played a sell-out concert at the Granby Halls in March.

A spokesman for the company dealing with the group, Jennie Halsall said: "Rainbow swore they would never take part in a festival such as this, but they have now agreed.

"They are doing it purely for the fans, and the money they receive for appearing is being ploughed straight back into the show", she added.

Apart from Rainbow, other leading heavy metal groups have been confirmed for the festival to be held on August 16.

The groups are Judas Priest, who like Rainbow, came to Leicester back in March, the Scorpions, April Wine, Riot and Touch.

Promoter Paul Loasby has promised a mystery act, which I understand may be American rock band Blue Oyster Cult.

POP by DAVE WATSON

Rainbow who are set to headline a major rock festival at Castle Donington next month, left to right: Ritchie Blackmore, Roger Glover, Don Airey, Cozy Powell and Graham Bonnet.

If the rock festival goes ahead, and arrangements with Donington Park are still to be finalised, then an estimated 60,000 rock fans could watch their favourites in action.

However the festival is still in doubt. Loughborough's M.P. Mr. Stephen Dorrell has expressed his concern. And Mr. Maurice Pettifor, Leicestershire's chief planner, said the Donington Park planning condition stated that no music should be relayed at the circuit on days other than pre-race and race days.

Large video screens will be mounted on each side of the stage to satisfy those not able to gain good vantage points.

A massive 40 kilowatt sound system will be backed by quadrophonic speaker towers at the corners of the audience.

Aircraft style spotlights are planned and a fireworks display may be another feature of a spectacular open-air event.

For those who prefer to stay in the comfort of their own home, plans are under way to film the festival for a television special.

The decision to hold a huge concert at Donington comes after complaints from rock fans that the Midlands have been missing out on open-air gigs.

London and the Home Counties and Scotland have been well catered for in recent years.

Now the Midlands with a wide catchment area will have their chance.

When I spoke to Jennie Halsall about fears from villagers about the proposed concert, she replied: "I can assure those people that before an event like this is put on, everything is looked into in the minutest detail.

"Catering, extra security and toilet facilities - all have to be approved and paid for by the promoter", she said.

"Promoter Paul Loasby has worked with Harvey Goldsmith to stage the Dylan concert at Blackbushe and the concert at Knebworth, so he certainly knows what he is doing.

"In my experience there has never been any trouble at a heavy metal festival, and the recent one at Loch Lomond was free of incidents."

In The Eyes Of The World

Even if the council had lost the battle, Leicestershire Police put in their preparations for Saturday 16th August. The *Leicester Mercury* reported that a band of drug squad officers would be making an appearance at the biggest music festival ever to be held in the Midlands. They were part of 844 uniformed and plain clothed police that would be patrolling Donington Park and preventing chaos on surrounding roads. 50,000 teenagers were expected.

A Leicester City FC home match and a caravan rally near East Midlands Airport coincided with the concert and Leicestershire Police were hard-pressed to find sufficient manpower. Extra support was brought in from Derbyshire and Nottinghamshire. Weekend leave was cancelled and most of the force had to work 12-hour shifts.

Chief Superintendent Cliff Kendrick said: "We

are not expecting trouble, but we will maintain a high level of police presence."

A mobile police station was set up on the race circuit and Castle Donington High School was turned into a police canteen for the day.

Although the organisers had stressed there was no camping the police were still expecting some fans would arrive to camp on the Friday evening.

****

For headliners Rainbow their appearance at the first Donington Festival is one of the most talked about events in the band's history. The folklore surrounding Donington is probably for a number of reasons.

Firstly, it was the first big festival Rainbow had played in the UK. Although the band had planned to appear as the main support to Queen at an open-air show at Cardiff Castle in September '76. They pulled out of that particular show, apparently because they were unable to use their full stage set-up with the illuminated Rainbow.

But by 1980, with *Down To Earth* proving to be a big seller throughout Europe and Japan and the two top ten singles establishing the band's new direction and heightened profile, this did come at a price.

'Since You Been Gone,' written by former Argent guitarist Russ Ballard, wasn't without its critics. Not just from the music journalists but also from within the band. Cozy Powell voiced his objections at what he saw was a cynical recording of such a commercial tune that was the antithesis of the hard rock he considered Rainbow represented.

Commercial singles or not, Rainbow was still definitely heavier on stage when the band started the US tour in September 1979—A series of arena dates supporting Blue Öyster Cult which saw a shortened hour-long set based around the LP and including 'Eyes Of The World,' 'All Night Long,' 'Love's No Friend,' and 'Lost In Hollywood.' Truncated versions of previous stage favourites 'Man On The Silver Mountain,' 'Long Live Rock 'n' Roll,' 'Catch The Rainbow' and an instrumental revisiting of 'Kill The King' were also performed.

But Powell's dissatisfaction with the way things were going came to a head and finally set the seal on his future with the group. It was mutually agreed that he would commit to the rest of the touring schedule prior to a replacement being found. It was then announced that his final show would be the Monsters of Rock festival.

Powell also promised a spectacular finale to his time with Rainbow. He had been a big part of the band's success and his departure signified a major turning point for the band. Much capital was made of the fact that it was to be Cozy Powell's last gig with the band.

Prior to that there was the matter of Loasby and Jones getting the whole thing together. Efforts were severely hampered by the heavy rains during the week leading up to the gig. The local TV news did a short piece on the eve of the show with an upbeat Loasby saying, "It's going very well thank you. We've caught up on the lost time through rain although the current forecast is for a little more rain unfortunately, so we are just praying at the moment."

With concerns that the rain might put off many fans from attending Loasby responded by saying, "...very confident indeed and advance sales are right on target at the moment."

The usual concerns whenever there is a large gathering were also addressed. Ten years earlier when Blackmore's former band Deep Purple played an outdoor gig at the author's hometown, local residents were concerned that "Bovver Boys" would show up and cause damage.

Fast forward to Donington in 1980 and regarding behaviour a police spokesman said, "We've got sufficient police available tomorrow to deal with any contingency that may arise. We are not expecting any particular drug squad problem at all. No excessive use of drugs and certainly not expecting any public order problems although if it did arise, we should deal with it." Then again, he was hardly likely to say anything to the contrary!

During this brief broadcast Rainbow vocalist Graham Bonnet was also interviewed. "...as long as the weather holds out of course. This is the first time I have done an outdoors thing like this so it will be interesting to see what happens. As long as no one goes up in flames I will be pleased. It looks like we've got a good crowd tomorrow."

With it being Cozy Powell's last show, Bonnet also commented, albeit tongue in cheek, "I don't know what we can expect from Cozy tomorrow. He might come on stage riding a moped. He threatens that, with a cash helmet, the whole bit. He threatens to ride out here and fall over by the microphone right next door to me. I don't know, he might do that — I hope so."

Bonnet's light-hearted but seemingly off the wall comment was probably as a result of an event that happened during the recording of *Down To Earth* at Le Château Pelly-de-Cornfeld in Southern France. With the château's swimming pool, drained of its water over the winter months that they were recording there, the playful prankster Powell thought it would be amusing to ride a moped inside the pool! Fortunately, the band's tour manager Colin Hart captured this amusing event with a photograph.

Although on camera Loasby showed confidence that everything would go ahead smoothly despite the dreadful weather, privately he felt differently. Something that he spoke about recently: "The amount of rain was unbelievable. I'd borrowed money personally to put on this show. The night before, at four in the morning when a monsoon is coming down in Castle Donington, I'm sitting there with a bottle of Scotch in my hand thinking: "This is the ultimate, the biggest disaster in the history of rock 'n' roll and I'm going to lose everything." Not that I had anything, but I was going to lose it anyway."

Whilst the weather was hampering arrangements for the gig, once again that loveable rogue Cozy Powell also put a spanner in the works. Efforts were made to install a state-of-the-art quadraphonic sound system to ensure maximum volume and sonic boost with promises of impeccable sound quality. Indeed, it performed impressively during rehearsals the week before the festival.

However, parallel to a Judas Priest soundcheck just days before the event, a test for the local council safety officers of Cozy's pyrotechnics resulted in an explosion heard some three miles away that blew out all the P.A and caused £18,000 worth of damage to Priest's set-up.

When I interviewed Rainbow's Don Airey a few years ago he recalled, "We arrived on the Thursday & this deluge had opened & there was so much mud it was incredible. Then Cozy was trying out his explosives and he blew the P.A out of the park really. So that was a bit of a disaster so, anyway, come the day there was still mud but it didn't rain."

Larry Hogan who was Sandy Slavin's drum tech from Riot was also present when the P.A blew up. "What I remember most was hanging out with Cozy Powell sitting on a road case on stage drinking Heineken pint cans. We didn't have those in the States. The fire Marshall was there to inspect the pyro tech and there was a count down, but I thought they were just testing the P.A. I'm sure Cozy thought the same because you could see the shock on his face. When the blast came it blew the cans right off the road case. I found out later that they used a double charge and the speakers blew right out of the cabinets. Thus, an all-night work order was put in place because all of the speakers had to be replaced, they had to have new speakers sent in from London. My ears rang for two days."

Fortunately, the replacement equipment arrived on site in the nick of time and Priest's day was saved. It's unknown if any insurance claim was put in for the damage although if it was, it's unlikely the cause was put down to Cozy Powell's pyros setting off explosions!

Powell merely retorted: "They—Priest— were not too pleased—there was a lot of swearing going on!"

The day before the gig Rainbow rehearsed at a soundcheck and for anyone who happened to be in the vicinity at the time they would have heard Blackmore tinkering around with 'Weiss Heim,' the glorious instrumental that had been taped during the European tour and released as the B-side to 'All Night Long.' But it was nothing more than a minute or so and rumours that they might perform it at the gig were just that—nothing more.

With the dramas over, show day was imminent. But would the dreadful weather that had cast a shadow over the preparations during the preceding week impact on the day? The eyes of the rock world were on Donington, all that was left was for the bands to put on a memorable show.

Rainbow win at Donnington

RAINBOW are to headline their first major British outdoor rock festival — the latest in an avalanche of heavy metal events.

Black Sabbath and Sammy Hagar have also been approached for the festival, which will be staged on August 16 at Castle Donnington Racecourse near Leicester.

The decision to stage the show follows a closely-fought tussle between two rival promoters trying to stage HM festivals on the same site within a week of each other.

One London promoter was trying to set up a metal marathon with Rush and Black Sabbath at Castle Donnington on August 23, but after several weeks of negotiating with the owners and licensees, Paul Loasby and Midland Concert Promotions secured the site for Rainbow on August 16.

Loasby is currently lining up six other HM bands for the Monsters Of Rock festival, and it is understood that Sabbath and Sammy Hagar are in line for the show.

The racecourse has space for about 60,000 people, and a coach service will shuttle fans from Derby and Nottingham stations to the site from 8am on August 16. Gates open at 10am, the music starts at 1pm with closedown planned for 10.30pm.

Tickets are available by post at £7.50 from PO Box 123, Walsall W55, 4QQ with an sae, and postal orders payable to Woolteare Ltd; and by personal application from Friday at the following outlets:

Birmingham Cyclops, Coventry Theatre, Leicester Revolver Records, Stafford and Leeds Virgin Records, Derby and Burton-on-Trent R.E. Cords, Nottingham Selectadisc, Stafford Lotus Records, Stoke Mike Lloyds, Wolverhampton Sundown Records, Bristol Rival Records, Newcastle City Hall, Carlisle Pink Panther, Oxford New Theatre, Southampton Gaumont, London Rainbow and Virgin Ticket Machine, Manchester Piccadilly Records, Liverpool Probe Records, Edinburgh Odeon, Glasgow Apollo and Cardiff Spillers Record.

Tickets on the day will cost £8.50.

Ritchie Blackmore — Rainbow's cantankerous "man in black" — blows a kiss to his admirer.

SOUNDS

Cozy Powell

End of Cozy's Rainbow

The heavy metal bonanza at Castle Donington next week will be the last Rainbow date for top drummer Cozy Powell.

Cozy has decided to leave Rainbow, who are topping the bill at the Monsters of Rock Festival, after the show on August 16.

Cozy gave in his notice during the band's U.S. tour last year, and has extended his stay slightly to take in the festival. His reason is that after five years, he wants a change.

The Festival, at Castle Donington racetrack, will be a first for Rainbow.

Keyboards player Don Airey explained: "We never wanted to do an open-air festival before, because we had all had such bad experiences with them in our other bands.

"But things are different now, and we chose the Midlands because it's a heavy rock stronghold."

The one-day festival will also feature Birmingham's heavy metal giants Judas Priest, German band Scorpions, April Wine, Saxon, Riot and Touch.

JACKIE BAILEY

I Guess You Know What You Wanna See

Touch will always go down in Monsters of Rock history as the first band to play at the festival. They had released their debut single in May and debut album the following month and they really were the fresh-faced new kids on the block.

As is often the case with festivals, being the first on the bill they seemed to go largely ignored. However, journalist Malcolm Dome, then writing for *Record Mirror* wrote retrospectively, "Tramping out to see openers Touch was something of a dual between mud-soaked boots and determined leg muscles. Still, the struggle was worth it. Up to a point. Now, Touch had made their impact earlier in the year with their quality, self-titled debut album. It's since become acknowledged as a melodic rock masterclass and got significant attention in 1980. But onstage in the open, things did not work out for them. The subtlety of their sound was lost in the swirl of the conditions. They needed a more enclosed environment to get across the songs, and a lot of the depth and layers to the music simply got swamped in a sound that was hardly pristine. They clearly played well, but this didn't cut through."

Sadly for Touch, their performance is best remembered for the drama surrounding bassist Doug Howard, who swallowed a bee on stage. "I had an open bottle of beer on the side of the stage, and a bee somehow got in. I took a gulp of beer without realising the bee was there, and it was still alive and stung me."

Howard was rushed to the emergency medical room on site where worried media crammed outside waiting for news. Touch's manager Bruce Payne made light of the escapade when he flippantly announced, "It was touch and go but the doc says the bee will pull through."

It was, however, more serious as Howard explained, "I had to be rushed to hospital because I had an allergic reaction to the bee sting. People now think it's funny, but it could have had serious consequences for me."

Touch was also hampered by the P.A. system which only seemed to work well for those few thousand crammed down the front of the stage. In fact, the supposedly state-of-the-art quadraphonic system was clearly lacking and presented problems all day.

****

Despite the sound, second band on the bill Riot appeared to do better in getting across to the crowd, thanks to a more in-your-face attitude. This was largely down to the energetic antics of frontman Guy Speranza and the New Yorkers delivered a far more convincing set. They won over a lot of new fans and Speranza felt the day was a highlight of the band's career.

Years later, guitarist Mark Reale said, "I think Riot was one of the handful of bands that were the USA's answer to the NWOBHM at that time period."

Larry Hogan recalls Donington with much affection: "I have many fond memories of this event. It was the first time I had left the U.S.A. I had worked with Sandy for four years by this time and it was a gift from Sandy and management to bring me along. It was cheaper to hire a tech when they got there so I appreciated it even more. Yes, I remember the mud, and all the hay bales but I also remember the size of the sticks Cozy played and all the sawdust around his kit when he was done. He played really hard. There was a picture of me coming up the high steps to the stage just before we went on carrying a spare pedal, sticks, and towels, I believe Ross Halfin was the photographer, I had really long hair and I stuck my tongue out at him. It made the inside sleeve of the live album. I haven't seen that picture in years."

As documented by Martin Popoff in his book *Swords And Tequila*, Riot's stand at Monsters of Rock was a definite trip, a career highlight.

"That was mindboggling," according to guitarist Rick Ventura, "because that was playing for a sea of people. It was just the ultimate experience. Probably one of the highlights of playing with Riot was doing that festival because the fans were just so enthusiastic. I don't think anything topped that. But it was a lot of political manoeuvring and negotiating by managers just to get us in there. I grew up on and was fascinated by British bands, so for me it was like going to heaven. Unbelievable experience. The fans just absolutely loved the band. That's all I can say. They were so into it and they just lived it."

"It was definitely an honour to be asked to be a part of history, being one of the very first metal festivals!" mused band leader Mark Reale, speaking with Patrick Prince. "Along with hard rockin' bands like Rainbow, Scorpions, Priest, April Wine and thousands strong, we were paving the way for bigger things to come in the metal community. We found that Europe really embraced the band and our sound. The soundtrack is legendary as well and our song 'Road Racin'' appearing on it was an honour. A lot of bands were up-and coming at the time. I think Riot was one of the handful of bands that were the USA's answer to the NWOBHM at that time period. We basically helped create the US version. I think we helped pave the way and acceptance for this type of music."

As Popoff wrote: "This was the inaugural of many Monsters of Rock (making it essentially a

Narita-era gig), with Riot and Touch playing baby band roles in support of Rainbow, Judas Priest, Scorpions, April Wine and Saxon, the latter of which stole the show—and then later hired Riot on as a support act. Riot in fact had been in the midst of the monolithic Black and Blue tour with Black Sabbath and Blue Öyster Cult and flew to England for the weekend and then back again to the states to resume their support duty to the sparring rock giants. Riot was considered good but not great at Donington, but to be fair, the guys were somewhat harried and spooked by arguments between management and the label, arguments which nearly got them scotched from the gig. Still, UK fans were surprised at how the possessor of that legendary power metal voice could be somewhat reticent in his role as front man."

"Back in '81, Cliff Dunn had asked Kip Leming about the experience, and why UK punters seemed to dig Riot. 'I think Riot has always had that little bit of English influence in the sense that we play a style very similar,' answered Leming. 'Our style is a lot like the feeling of British metal in the way that it is not prepared, but rather spontaneous when we are in concert. The English like their metal hard and heavy without the feeling that they're being put on. Some bands put on a show with all the lights, explosions and choreographed movements, and that really turns the British off because they feel they're being dazzled by the show rather than the music.'"

Again, from *Swords And Tequila* "Well, it was my first festival, and it was the first Monsters of Rock festival, yes," affirmed Reale. "That was a trip. I met Bobby Rondinelli for the first time, backstage, because Richie was grooming him to replace Cozy, who was leaving after that."

****

If Riot had... err... a riot at Donington then so did Saxon. The Yorkshire band's forty-five-minute set cut through with the audience, many of whom were far more familiar with their material than the two New York bands that had preceded them.

Frontman Biff Byford lapped up the day: "It was great! It was of course the first major festival of the eighties and we were the young bloods on there. Everyone else was really big and established, Scorpions, Priest, Rainbow. We just went up there and stormed it... it was magnificent. Fantastic feeling. When we walked on that stage we'd done a hundred thousand records. I would imagine that ninety-nine per cent of the people in that audience had got *Wheels Of Steel*. So, it was fantastic for us. It was our first festival gig, the first time we'd played to an audience of over three thousand. The roar when we went out on stage was incredible. When I walked off I thought: 'Follow that.' That was a fucking great gig."

Biff Byford: "This was the new generation of heavy metal. This was our music — fucking have it!

After so many years in the doldrums, British rock now seemed unstoppable."

As documented in Martin Popoff's book *Denim And Leather*, Byford adds, "People won't forget it, and obviously the memories are there all the time. It was the first outdoor festival we played. We were like the new kids on the block on that festival. Rainbow, Priest, Scorpions... I suppose for April Wine it was sort of their first big gig as well, and Riot. But there was really only us and Maiden and Def Leppard that hadn't had any real radio or TV success. So, when we had walked on stage, I think a lot of people were quite shocked at how big we were, actually."

As Popoff says, "Biff figures the band had played about sixty gigs in the ramp-up to Donington, already rising from the clubs through the civic halls, and arriving in front of 60,000 fans to what amounts to a hero's welcome."

Byford again: "It was our very first roll of success there, with *Wheels of Steel*, and it was just a snapshot of what was happening in England. People were into us, weren't they? So, it's a good snapshot of what the '80s thing was, especially for a lot of the younger fans, and obviously through the recordings, for people abroad who weren't there. But I think they were all surprised as to our popularity. Ritchie was having a great gig; he was in a great mood. But shortly after that we went out with Judas Priest in Europe, which was our first European tour. So yeah, it was a great time, and a milestone for the New Wave of British Heavy Metal, because it was the first time that a band from it, like us, got to play in front of 60,000 people, really, to play our style of music, which was a lot more aggressive, a lot more sort of working class audience-oriented, rather than superstars playing long solos and things."

Aside from the actual performance, new boys Saxon also enjoyed mingling with the many other rockers in the backstage area. Being the first major festival of the eighties and the first devoted to heavy rock, it was full of rock dignitaries, including many from the new bands such as Def Leppard's Joe Elliot and Iron Maiden's Steve Harris. Representing the old guard were such guitarists as Uriah Heep's Mick Box and Michael Schenker. The latter presumably there to watch Scorpions but quite probably to also lure Cozy Powell, who joined his band soon after the event.

****

Canadian rockers April Wine arguably had a tough act to follow. For Malcolm Dome, their set didn't really cut it. "Saxon's strength was put into even more perspective by a rather lame appearance from Canada's April Wine. They really weren't suited to the braggadocio of the beer bravado brigade out front. What was needed was a little more power and punch than the Winos could deliver. It wasn't that their performance lacked sparkle... no, actually it was exactly that. Their cover of King Crimson's '21st Century Schizoid Man' was decent, but when Myles Goodwin fashioned the crowd into shouting out "I like to rock," and then tried to pretend the band would play the song of the same title due to demand, it was embarrassing."

In the balance of fair play, one man's meat and all that… Don Airey thought April Wine was outstanding.

****

For most of the audience the next three bands were the star attractions. Scorpions had a strong fan base already in the UK, not easy for a German band in a market dominated by home-grown and American acts where English is the native language. Whilst Scorpions sung in English as well, vocalist Klaus Meine didn't have the greatest command of the language. Even though he shrieked "Hello Donning Castle!" at the start of the performance, Scorpions were for many the best band of the day.

Although their latest album, *Animal Magnetism* had been released in March, the set was still largely based around the previous record, *Lovedrive* that had really cemented the Scorps in the UK.

From the *UK Rock Festivals* website Andy White said. "To me the Scorpions were playing as well as they ever did at that time in their career (prior to the MTV-friendly version we got a few years later) and their set was as faultless as ever (I saw them three times during 1980). I recall 'Pictured Life' being a particular favourite of mine at the time."

****

Having overcome the destruction of their equipment at the hands of the pyrotechnics, Judas Priest delivered in all their pomp and Priest was riding high on the back of the *British Steel* album released in April.

Once again Malcolm Dome retrospectively nails it: "Judas Priest were a killer name to have second on the bill. The *British Steel* album was flying high, and the Priest's stock had never been stronger. NWOBHM had brought them right into focus, and they weren't about to pass up the chance to pound the world—well, Donington—like a battering ram. They began with an overwrought version of 'Hell Bent For Leather,' before sliding into 'The Ripper' and 'Running Wild.' It was a stunning affirmation of Priest's pre-eminence, and when Rob Halford rode a Harley onstage, it got everyone roaring with delight. Incredibly, while the band played 'Living After Midnight,' they didn't do 'Breaking The Law' from the *British Steel* record. But nobody cared. We got 'Sinner,' 'Grinder,' 'Victim Of Changes' and 'Tyrant.' This was hardcore Judas Priest style heavy metal!"

As Dome points out, they omitted one of the obvious tracks from *British Steel*. In fact, they only played three from the album, with the rest of the set made up of a strong selection of material that spanned across the previous four records from 1978's *Killing Machine* and *Stained Class* to 1977's *Sin After Sin* and *Sad Wings Of Destiny* from '76.

Only the debut album *Rocka Rolla* got ignored. In all, Priest delivered a set that impressed and delivered to the hordes of devotees as K.K Downing acknowledged: "I was very nervous beforehand. I was terrified I might break a string! But after the first song, my nerves went. The fans were so clearly with us. A great day."

On his website, Downing recalls Donington as a high point of his career: "Well, I guess I was one of the lucky ones. What more could I have asked for in 1980, it was a dream come true. To be a special guest at Donington and with such great names and some of my favourite bands I felt that Priest had truly arrived.

"The day started with yours truly being very nervous, how would it go, would I play well? Would I break a string? Would my guitar stay in tune? My head was just spinning with excitement. I remember arriving in the artist's car park and seeing familiar faces immediately: some kicking football, some talking to attractive girls, others just chilling and having a cigarette and a beer. I was amidst the rock giants of the time.

"The sun was shining and everything looked perfect, the crowd of fans seemed to go on for ever, the thunderous applause for the bands one after the other gave me chills, although it meant that

Priest had to come out fighting like never before.

"The light started to fade. It was our turn, we hit the stage with a vengeance, and the whole place seemed to vibrate in time. After the first song had gone so did any of my nerves, it seemed we could do no wrong the fans were with us.

"We played as good as we possibly could. Before I knew, it was time for the last song. I seem to remember it all went so fast, I wanted to keep playing. We had so many songs we could have played, but our time was up. We had to make way for the mighty Rainbow, but the crowd cheered on.

"This was England, this was metal, and this was Donington—the festival I will never forget."

Andy White watched Priest's set in an unusual fashion: "I remember getting into a queue for a burger approximately twenty minutes prior to Judas Priests' set and still being stood in the same place in the queue some one and a half hours later after they had left the stage. I think the stallholder must have been a Priest fan!"

****

One thing that most of the crowd was probably unaware of was the significant distance between the stage and the dressing room area. Bands, crew and journalists were routinely ferried in little buses and golf-like carts to and fro all day long.

Saxon's Graham Oliver recalled: "I took a shuttle bus to backstage to watch Judas Priest with

Joe Elliott, who was there ligging. As I walked to the stage, a Mercedes car with black windows was parked nearby and the window came down to a shout of "Graham! Graham!" I turned to look and I thought, "It's fucking Ritchie Blackmore! He knew my name!" He called me over to the car and greeted me like an old mate. I was blown away! We talked about guitars and he said he'd seen Hendrix at the Isle Of Wight fest. He thanked me for a comment about him in a music mag, where I'd stated that he was a great influence, and I told him that the intro I wrote for 'See The Light Shining' was inspired by the intro to the *Made In Japan* version of 'Highway Star.' Ritchie laughed… I bet he said… "ripped me off!"

Oliver's memory may have slightly got the better of him. Either that or Blackmore was delivering one of his infamous wind-ups as it was impossible for him to have seen Hendrix at the Isle of Wight in 1970. Hendrix was billed for 30th August. The same day Blackmore with Deep Purple was gigging at the Civic Centre, Pasadena in the States. Even allowing for the fact that Hendrix's set was delayed and he didn't actually perform until the early hours of the 31st, given the time difference between the UK and America, Blackmore would have required a time machine of H.G Wells' proportions in order to achieve such a claim!

Moot point aside, despite the successful performances that had already occurred at

Donington, the main attraction was still to come.

****

In truth only Rainbow and Judas Priest could be considered at the time as "monsters of rock" and Scorpions, although gaining in popularity were still someway to reaching their commercial peak with 'Winds Of Change.' The other bands were generally groups on the way up or in the case of some of them, on the way out!

With an anticipated audience of 50,000 and plans to record the concert, Blackmore had naturally wanted to ensure Rainbow was well prepared for the event.

Three warm-up shows in Scandinavia on the 8th, 9th and 10th of August preceded it and some changes to the set were made.

Rainbow's most popular song 'Stargazer' was reintroduced, but in a much shorter version than had been performed on the Rising tour in 1976. In Malmö the open-air gig was interrupted by rain, so the band departed for the hotel during Airey's keyboard solo!

In press interviews Blackmore hinted at some surprises in store for the concert, though plans to fly Ritchie on a high wire over the heads of the audience during the show were abandoned when the hoist machine failed.

Part of the huge stage set included two thirty-foot canvases depicting the artwork of the first two

Rainbow albums, and these were later offered as prizes in the weekly music paper *Sounds*. It would be fascinating to know who won them, and more importantly what they did with them as they were clearly too large to hang on a bedroom wall or indeed hang on the outside of a home unless the winners happened to live in tower blocks!

A twenty-four-page programme was produced for the event. Judas Priest had four pages devoted to them, whilst bizarrely headliners Rainbow had just three that included a small amount of text by *Melody Maker's* Steve Gett. It included a mention of Rainbow's tour of Japan three months earlier, with Gett saying the tour caused "more of an explosion than the H-bomb on Hiroshima." It could hardly be construed as one of the most sensitive comments ever written! Although the text was written a few weeks before the event, Gett also said "the weathermen were promising us a hot August" but this proved to be far from accurate.

As already mentioned, torrential rain over the preceding week had turned the site into a quagmire. The day itself dawned bright, hot and sunny. Thankfully the prevailing conditions didn't seem to put the fans off and a crowd of over 35,000 was officially reported-this may have been to satisfy fire regulations as unofficial estimates put the crowd at more than 50,000.

The Rainbow road crew turned up on the day with T-shirts specially printed proudly proclaiming to groupies "No head—No backstage passes!"

A few hours before going on stage, Richard Skinner interviewed Cozy Powell for BBC Radio 1's Saturday afternoon rock show and Cozy explained why he was leaving, "The band has been very successful for the last five years and Ritchie and I have had our differences in the past as you probably know. I wouldn't say we've had a lot of differences about the last year but I wasn't particularly happy with the last Rainbow album. I thought it was a bit too commercial. But that's all been aired in the press so I won't go on about it now but they're just about to start recording another new album if you believe all the rumours. But I want to do something different. I've been with the band for five years. I've figured it's time... if I'm going to leave I might as well leave at a gig like this. I want to do a few different things. I'm sure Ritchie's sick and tired of me moaning and groaning at him so I'll give him the chance to get somebody else in so he can moan and groan at somebody else. Halfway through the last American tour we had a little bit of a contretemps, and I said enough is enough. I knocked it on the head then and I told him then I'll be leaving after the European and Japanese dates, but I don't think they took me seriously. So, it was only a couple of weeks ago that they realised I was serious. So here we are today, the last gig: Donington racecourse, couldn't be better."

Cozy concluded by saying he had no regrets whatsoever about his decision. Cozy's replacement had already been lined up and Bobby Rondinelli

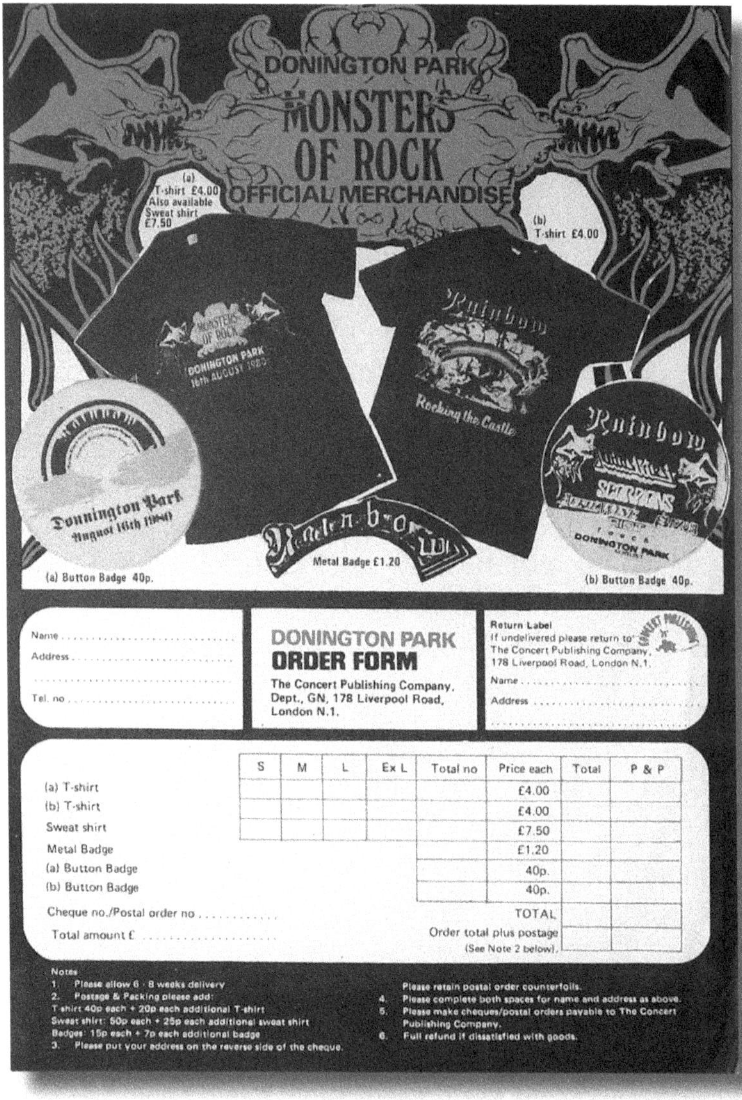

DONINGTON PARK
MONSTERS OF ROCK
OFFICIAL MERCHANDISE

(a) T-shirt £4.00
Also available Sweat shirt £7.50

(b) T-shirt £4.00

Metal Badge £1.20

(a) Button Badge 40p.

(b) Button Badge 40p.

Name ....
Address ....
....
Tel. no ....

DONINGTON PARK
ORDER FORM
The Concert Publishing Company, Dept., GN, 178 Liverpool Road, London N.1.

Return Label
If undelivered please return to:
The Concert Publishing Company, 178 Liverpool Road, London N.1.
Name ....
Address ....

	S	M	L	Ex L	Total no	Price each	Total	P & P
(a) T-shirt						£4.00		
(b) T-shirt						£4.00		
Sweat shirt						£7.50		
Metal Badge						£1.20		
(a) Button Badge						40p.		
(b) Button Badge						40p.		
						TOTAL		
						Order total plus postage (See Note 2 below).		

Cheque no./Postal order no ....
Total amount £ ....

Notes
1. Please allow 6 - 8 weeks delivery
2. Postage & Packing please add:
T-shirt 40p each + 20p each additional T-shirt
Sweat shirt: 50p each + 25p each additional sweat shirt
Badges: 15p each + 7p each additional badge
3. Please put your address on the reverse side of the cheque.
Please retain postal order counterfoils.
4. Please complete both spaces for name and address as above.
5. Please make cheques/postal orders payable to The Concert Publishing Company.
6. Full refund if dissatisfied with goods.

flew in from New York to catch the show. As Bobby explained, some people were of the opinion that his presence was not a good idea, "It was kind of silly because they didn't want me to run into Cozy. He was leaving anyway and I knew he knew I was there. It was like wherever he goes, "oh go the other way" I really felt like a dummy. I just wanted to go up and say "hi how are you doing" you know. But we became friends later. But I was at that gig because they wanted me to see the band live, which I'd already done in the States anyway."

Rainbow biographer Roy Davies is as good as anyone in assessing Rainbow's performance that day: After a lengthy ninety-minute wait (what would be a tiresome precursor of all future MOR festivals) the exquisite expectation built by the slowly burning intro of 'Eyes Of The World' never failed to raise the hairs on the neck; about as impressive an opener for a festival headliner as you could get. As the crowd got used to the layout and full headliner-approved sound it was immediately clear the mix was now all over the place, though by the time of the slow blues that is 'Love's No Friend' it was slowly improving. The song had on the prior tour inspired Blackmore to his most emotive work, and on the night itself was no exception, recalling memories of his solo flights on 'Mistreated' during the Dio era. A nice touch was Ritchie's subtle mimicking on guitar of Bonnet's vocal line.

The first of the 'hits' was got out of the way quickly and painlessly; 'Since You Been Gone' was

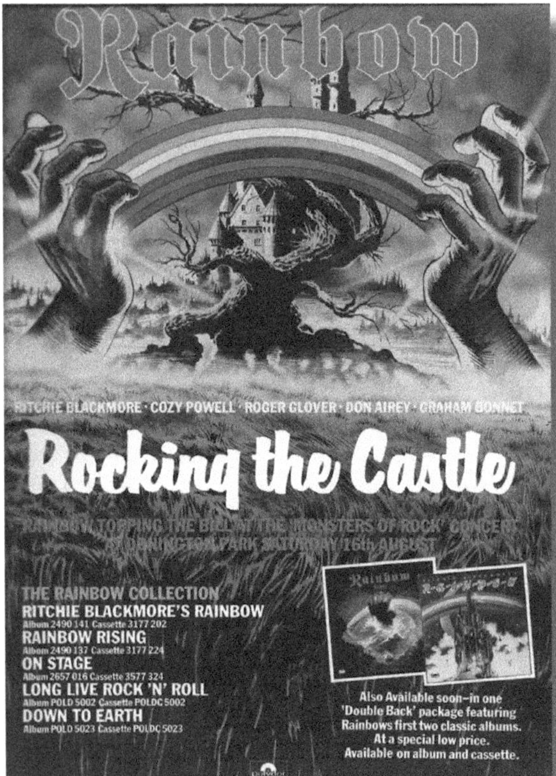
Rainbow
RITCHIE BLACKMORE · COZY POWELL · ROGER GLOVER · DON AIREY · GRAHAM BONNET
Rocking the Castle
THE RAINBOW COLLECTION
RITCHIE BLACKMORE'S RAINBOW
Album 2490 141 Cassette 3177 202
RAINBOW RISING
Album 2490 137 Cassette 3177 224
ON STAGE
Album 2657 016 Cassette 3577 324
LONG LIVE ROCK 'N' ROLL
Album POLD 5002 Cassette POLDC 5002
DOWN TO EARTH
Album POLD 5023 Cassette POLDC 5023
Also Available soon–in one
'Double Back' package featuring
Rainbows first two classic albums.
At a special low price.
Available on album and cassette.

featured, but in rather throwaway form, as if the whole band wanted to crack on with more satisfying fare. Here was the first obvious indication that Bonnet on stage was not the Bonnet on record, his phrasing on the chorus breathless and awkward. Bonnet's performance at the time seemed powerful and with (albeit nervous) gusto, particularly on the new material that suited his throaty bellow better than some of the Dio era tracks in the set list. Listening these days to the recordings of the show the overall impression is one where the singer often appeared stranded and out of his depth compared to the paid-my dues sleek professionalism of the other three in the band, who quickly picked up on Blackmore's improvisational twists and turns with the normal set.

The specially reinstated Dio-era epic 'Stargazer' also reprised earlier times, although unaided by orchestral accompaniment and without Dio's clarity the song sounded painfully thin. Concerns over Bonnet's shouted vocal attack were overcome by Ritchie's sonic solo. Indeed, the star of the show was still without doubt Blackmore, his guitar piece during the likes of 'Catch The Rainbow' simply sublime (If you ignore the intrusive aircraft noise from East Midlands airport!—picture several hundred plastic bottles being hurled at the rapidly ascending culprit!)
For perhaps the first time too a Rainbow keyboard player enjoyed equal billing sound-wise with the Man in Black, with the distinctive slant and colour

of Don Airey's keyboard parts central to filling out the band's rhythmic dynamic behind Glover's practised, sparing and undemonstrative bass lines.

The lengthy 'Lost In Hollywood' show-cased for one last time Cozy's '1812 Overture' drum solo — one of the lasting images of the day and the definitive showstopper.

'All Night Long' (Bonnet's hackneyed audience participation segment apart—bring on the mushy peas indeed!) fared a touch better than its sister hit, at least in a festival environment. The dynamic of the set dropped noticeably with the obligatory 'Blues' and 'Will You Love Me Tomorrow' though thankfully Blackmore's blast back into 'Long Live Rock 'n Roll' lifted the tempo at just the right time. The set was rounded off with a full and expected Stratocaster trashing, a Marshall stack cremation and a very striking (and reportedly very expensive) fireworks display.

Overall, Rainbow's 104-minute performance was not among their very best, but the recordings of the show reinforce there were occasional indications of their instrumental potency and latent power. There was undoubted potential of what was still after all a relatively new line-up; had Bonnet done another album / tour, assimilated himself into the creative loop and honed his stagecraft a little more and had Powell remained as Ritchie's sounding board for ideas, then the indications were all there that the quintet could have gone on and progressed more satisfactorily down the commercial path Ritchie had chosen.

The much-vaunted P.A. system only seemed to work well for those few thousand crammed down the front of the stage, anything above the slightest breeze carrying off the sound for the remainder of the crowd and with it any true sense of the band's considerable on-stage power.

But minor criticisms apart, the camaraderie and togetherness felt on the day meant the occasion was deemed an overwhelming success. From the organiser's point of view, they had lost money but had proved the principle sufficiently to have the confidence to organise a festival for the following year. Within a few short years it became the annual event for the UK hard rock fraternity, superseding the rival Reading Festival. The event was destined to become a British music tradition for over a decade and was eventually extended to include a list of dates through mainland Europe as well.

The metal monsters

Rainbow top the big rock festival bill

RAINBOW warriors ... (left to right) Ritchie Blackmore, Roger Glover, Don Airey, Cozy Powell and Graham Bonnet.

POPeye exclusive by Paul Cole

Not too many big-league rock bands would relish the near-suicidal prospect of following Judas Priest live on stage in their Midlands home-ground. Rainbow just love the idea.

Ritchie Blackmore's Rainbow warriors top the bill at next Saturday's Donington "Monsters of Rock" festival – with the Black Country supergroup in the support slot.

It's probably the first time in years Priest have played support to anyone in the Midlands – and it could mean a right royal battle of the bands.

Rainbow keyboardsman Don Airey told me of the reasons for risking the wrath of hardened Judas Priest fans – and of the many moods of temperamental Ritchie – rock's Man In Black.

He told, too, of his reactions to claims that heavy rockers Rainbow sold out with their last album — packed with punchy commercial rock.

Said Don: "We weren't too sure that Rob Halford and the lads in Judas Priest would play support — even though Roger Glover helped produce them at one stage.

"We wanted very much to get them because they provide a great contrast to our own music, and they'll make us work hard. The Priest sound sets our own off nicely.

"Added to that is the fact that they're probably the biggest band in the Midlands right now, and a lot of their fans will get a good chance to see them in action at home.

"We sent out special invitations to Judas Priest, Scorpions and Saxon to join us on the bill, and the promoters sorted out the rest."

Life in Rainbow can be notoriously difficult. Since former Deep Purple guitarist Ritchie formed the band, he's hired and fired enough musicians to fill the unemployment gap.

Don was one of the latest additions, joining ex-Purples Ritchie and Roger Glover after a spell with the magnificent Colosseum II. It wasn't at all easy.

"Ritchie can be difficult and demanding," says Don. "You have to keep on your toes all the time or you might find you're no longer in the band.

"Ritchie tries to get the band sounding as good as humanly possible. When I was with Colosseum some of my equipment didn't always use to work on stage.

"In Rainbow everything has to be in perfect order and condition. He's a perfectionist who's quite a nice guy on the quiet."

Rainbow's recent hit singles success in the charts led to cries of "Sell Out" from some of the fans, but Don denies the band have ever been anything but heavy rock 'n' roll.

"The Down To Earth album that the singles were from could have been an absolute shambles," he said. "It was our first album with the new line-up and was done pretty quickly.

"Ritchie pulled us all together and the album contained some good commercial rock songs. It was a bit restricted and we're now into more serious music.

We've been looking at more extended pieces, and the next album will be much more raunchy with more technical playing. At the same time it will still be good hard rock 'n' roll music."

The big Midland festival will be the last-ever appearance of Cozy Powell as the drummer of Rainbow.

Cozy left semi-retirement and a motor racing career to join the band five years ago — and looks likely to return to his first love within the next few weeks.

Said Cozy today: "The Donington Festival will be my last appearance with Rainbow. I gave my notice in last year, but agreed to play until the end of the European tour. Donington will be my last gig with the band."

Ritchie Blackmore said of the resignation: "Cozy and I have been together for a really good five years and I wish him nothing but success in his future ventures."

How they will line-up

The Castle Donnington "Monsters of Rock" festival is the heaviest of them all — with an ear-splitting 80,000 watts of sound to prove the point.

The superstar rock-fest kicks off at 1 p.m. on Saturday, August 16 at the Castle Donnington Racing Circuit in Leicestershire — and runs all night. The megawatt monsters of rock, in order of appearance will be:

TOUCH — the latest Total Rock import from the States playing their first ever UK gig after a finely crafted debut album with all the promise of a new Boston.

RIOT — heavy metal merchants who debuted with the classic Riot City album, a blockbuster set of short, sharp rock songs.

SAXON — Britain's latest heavy rock heroes currently charting with strong commercial hard rock after a meteoric rise to fame, and hit singles Wheels of Steel and 747 Strangers in the Night.

APRIL WINE — French Canada's rock superstars in a surprisingly high place on the bill after just one UK tour. About the most laid-back band on the bill, with the emphasis on high-volume melody and skill.

SCORPIONS — Germany's answer to the energy crisis, playing blisteringly hot rock 'n' Roll with all the subtlety of a train crash. You either love them or hate them. I prefer a headache.

JUDAS PRIEST — Rob Halford's heavy band aiming to blow Rainbow off-stage after their best-ever album British Steel. They're doing the same thing supporting Ted Nugent very soon in a European rock festival.

RAINBOW — now firmly entrenched in the Rock Monster league with all the power and passion that entails. They've proved they can play heavy and light — and are now moving to more ambitious things.

Gates at Donnington open at 10 a.m. and there are special buses arranged from Birmingham and other Midlands towns. A special phone service to deal with all enquiries from fans is on Walsall 33310.

Down To Colin

Rainbow's tour manager Colin Hart gave his account of Donington in his own autobiography A Hart Life *published in 2011.*

Back home in Connecticut, plans were being made between Bruce and promoter Paul Loasby for Rainbow to headline a massive "Monsters of Rock" open-air event at Castle Donington in August, just two months away. Timing being Cozy's forte, he announced to the band that he would quit after that show, a fitting finale to a great partnership with Ritchie and Roger. It had been brewing for months; Cozy just did not want to be in a singles chart band and all that that brought with it. He wanted to be part of a band that had massive album success as he thought that gave him more credibility as a musician. Singles success, he thought, made him look, well, cheap and of no substance—a peddler of three and a half minute 'ditties.'

The supporting line-up at Donington was to be Judas Priest, our German chums the Scorpions, Saxon, Canadian rockers April Wine, Riot and one of Bruce's protégés Touch. After three warm up dates in Scandinavia with Touch, we arrived in London where we would be based. With Ray D'Addario as our production manager ensuring all the equipment was available, I set about making plans for the band to get on site, which was never easy as, like Purple before them and I guess any major band, they all had their own agendas and preferences on a show like this. Roger wanted to experience the whole thing and see all the bands whilst Ritchie wanted to get there his usual thirty-five minutes before show time, do the old Johnnie Walker Black Label whisky routine, hit the stage, do the show and fuck off. Cozy, as it was his last show, wanted to make it spectacular and had devised a massive firework and pyrotechnic show during his drum solo of the 1812 overture, so he wanted to be there during the set up and sound check.

This meant me almost running a limo taxi service from our base at the Holiday Inn, Swiss Cottage, London and the festival site, some hundred miles up the M1 motorway. Cozy, as ever the self-sufficient, level-headed guy said he'd get himself there, leaving me to concentrate on the others. However, I did arrange to be present when Cozy 'rehearsed' his explosions! He wanted the biggest explosion the pyro guys could muster for the finale, so he asked them to demonstrate how loud they could get it from a buried steel pipe. Well, for a radius of five miles, mothers gave birth, hens lay early and to some, World War Three had started, so loud was the explosion. So loud in fact it blew out about twenty speakers of the brand-new Quadraphonic PA, literally tearing the cones. They were not best pleased. Cozy, however, smiling broadly said it would do just fine. The road crews then spent a hectic four hours replacing the speakers. It had just not occurred to anybody to set the explosion behind the stage, as it would be on the night and where it would not harm the PA, instead preferring the easier option front of stage.

The show was taped, so at last Rainbow were getting the exposure they deserved although the critics were less than complementary, but as Led Zeppelin were no strangers to this type of criticism either, most thought we kept good company. The festival sold out, the crowds were ecstatic and they were the ultimate barometer of whether we were 'cutting the mustard.' It was sad afterwards, saying goodbye to Cozy. He had driven the band, stood up to Ritchie and, with Roger, in my opinion, had provided an unequalled powerhouse and platform for Ritchie. I know he thought the world of Cozy, but, as always, did not know how to say so. Perhaps he had more pressing, personal problems on his mind?

This really was the age of heavy metal. Some

Rock music goes on trial at race circuit

Rock music at Castle Donington race track goes on trial with a Heavy Metal spectacular next Saturday.

For the all-day event, featuring top HM bands Rainbow and Judas Priest (pictured), is to be monitored by district and county council officials for its noise and nuisance value.

The Rock Monster Show begins at 1.0 p.m. and runs until 10.30 p.m., featuring seven bands and costing £7.50 in advance and £8.50 on the door.

For Heavy Metal fans it represents quite a tasty fare with Scorpions, April Wine, Saxon, Riot and Touch making up the other five performers.

INVESTIGATED

And Castle Donington managing director, Mr Peter Gaydon, is confident of success. "Donington Circuit is delighted to be able to host this fantastic event. It will be the first occasion that a motor racing circuit has ever moved into the field of rock and we hope Castle Donington will become a top venue in the future.

"We have investigated thoroughly the regulations that govern all events at Donington and we have taken legal advice from the very highest levels. The results of those investigations show conclusively that Donington is perfectly entitled to hold such an event," he said.

Local residents and parish councils were not so sure. The prospect of a day of loud music and some 60,000 rock fans pouring into the circuit led to complaints.

Both North West Leicestershire District Council and Leicestershire County Council considered the complaints and investigated what steps, if any, ought to be taken.

CONCERNS

District Planning Officer Mr Christopher North said: "At the end of the day the district council felt because the race track was designed for large crowds there were no highway causes or general planning reasons to prevent it being held."

There was concern about the noise but this could not really be gauged until the event had taken place so members had decided to see whether any problems arose from this first event.

"The county came to much the same conclusions and we are monitoring the event, particularly in terms of noise. Both councils will be represented there to see how it goes," he said.

SHUTTLE

So both bands and fans will be on trial but it is doubtful whether either will let this spoil the fun.

The gates will be open from 10 a.m. onwards and there will be a shuttle service from both Derby and Nottingham stations from 8 a.m. onwards.

Advance tickets are available locally from R.E. Cords at both Burton and Derby.

weeks after Donington, The Reading Festival was dominated by UFO, Def Leppard, Iron Maiden, David and Whitesnake and Wishbone Ash. Sales of hairspray and calls for hair dryers tripled in London hotels overnight! I wondered at the time if we had maybe done the wrong festival, as I'm sure Ritchie would have fancied his chances at Reading. The challenge to blow that bill off the stage would have been mouth-watering. Ritchie lived for challenges such as that would have presented, as it brought the very best (and worst) out of him. I have no doubt there would have been a conversation on the subject between him and Bruce. The ghosts of the past shimmered in our consciousness in that August of 1980 when the compilation album *Deepest Purple* went to No.1 in the UK charts, a welcome reminder to Ritchie in the current climate of change that a reunion could always be an option.

Bobby Rondinelli had already been lined up, after yet more exhaustive auditions back in Long Island, to replace Cozy and was at Donington to see what he'd taken on. He had been flown over, met the crew, spent time with the ever-accommodating Cozy and then flew back with Ritchie and Roger and myself to America where he lived close to us all, a native of Long Island. Bobby was a skilful basher in the Cozy, 'Bonzo' Bonham mould and would fit in really well, I hoped, for his sake as well as mine. I was getting fed up with this constant 'getting to know you' routine. Too late, in September we went to Copenhagen to begin the next album and it all started to go pear shaped with our Mr. Bonnet.

From *A Hart Life* by Colin Hart with Dick Allix, ISBN: 978-1-908724-04-5

Broken Dreams In The Ground

All told, this first attempt at something new was an unqualified success. Despite the rain from the previous week, the sunshine on the day played its part.

Richard Whitehead, writing for the *Atherstone News and Herald* gave his detailed account of events: "The writer who penned those immortal lines 'Mud, mud glorious mud' must have had something like the scene at Castle Donington in mind when he chewed on his nib in search of inspiration. Despite the rays of golden sunshine that, thankfully, lit up the day the rain that had fallen throughout the week had taken its toll on the site of this heavy metal extravaganza. Everywhere the eye roamed there was mud. The whole field was a sea of thick, black morass and thousands of denim clad fans wallowed in it like contented hippos in a jungle swamp.

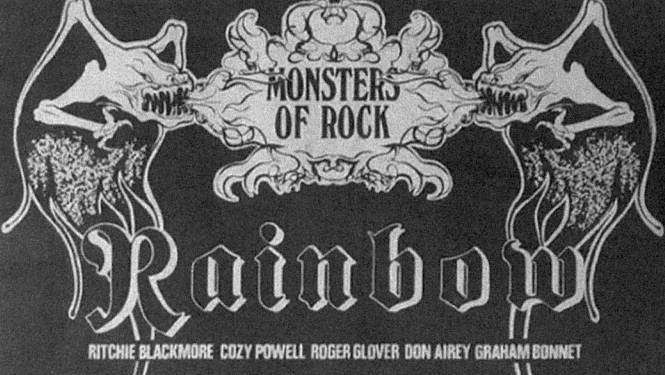

"Seven bands offering varying degrees of metallic mayhem were on view in what had been billed as the biggest celebration of the heavy rock 'genre' ever staged in this country. Many were still arriving and most were strolling around the site perimeter when the opening band Touch took to the stage. Competent if not very inspiring. Touch hadn't had the benefit of a sound check and on their UK debut they must have won themselves a few friends even if they did drift off into Stateside Dollar rock at intervals. After that we decided to escape the quagmire that was the festival site for the relative calm of the dressing rooms and bar area. The absence of the usual press enclosure alarmed many of the national reporters who were a little aggrieved at having to "muck in" with the paying customers.

"Riot arrived and duly departed for the stage in breakneck fashion. Saxon, probably the most popular of the New Wave of heavy metal bands, rolled up and adjourned to their dressing rooms to re-appear wearing trousers that looked as if they had been sprayed on.

"After Saxon, the maple leaf of Canada was raised for April Wine, who attracted a lot of attention on their first visit to this country in February. Despite the Canadian origin April Wine's music is firmly rooted in the American market for they line up with three guitarists yet still manage to sound lightweight and poppy at times.

"Back at the dressing rooms April Wine were

giving nothing away. whether this meant they were unhappy with their performance or whether they were trying to look like big stars I'm not sure.

"After that it was celebrities all the way. First the Scorpions, looking very German and, as singer Klaus Meine admitted, very nervous, drove up in large Mercedes. Just after the Scorpions arrived Michael Schenker strode on to the scene looking in the rudest of health. Drugs and booze ruined this brilliant guitarist's career with UFO but now he is preparing to return to the British stage next month, he is taking no chances, a bottle of spa water stayed firmly in his grasp all afternoon.

"Rainbow bassist Roger Glover chatted amiably with everyone. He told me they were looking forward to the gig and that the soundcheck had gone very well. Whitesnake guitarist Bernie Marsden was on the scene as was Uriah Heep man Ken Hensley.

"Later, after the ridiculously dressed Judas Priest had left for their thrash, Cozy Powell and Graham Bonnet of Rainbow merged from their nearby hotel. This was to be Powell's last appearance for Rainbow and questions about his future met with non-committal answers. That only left Ritchie Blackmore and as the controversial Man in Black had been staying at a different hotel from the rest of the band it was difficult to predict his arrival. When he did make his appearance, it took everyone by surprise for his chauffeur driven car swept into the car park, the great man looked contemptuously at everyone and the car drove away again.

"The crowd had grown impatient for Rainbow to appear down on the arena and understandably tempers were a little fraught when the taped 'Pomp and Circumstance' intro boomed out over the monster of a PA.

"We had been promised special effects in abundance and by golly that was what we got. Two huge paintings of the covers of the first two Rainbow albums flanked the stage and the massive video screen gave a sometimes-fascinating view of the band on stage.

"Under a colossal lighting rig Rainbow played what may not have been their best ever set but the sheer overwhelming grossness of everything left everyone spellbound. Overblown is the only way to describe it.

"Blackmore was cocooned in a world all of his own. Occasionally he would become aware of the audience and when he did, he danced around and waved his arm.

"It's impossible to tell what is going through this great musician's mind. I doubt that anyone will ever get to the bottom of his spine-chilling character, but he is without doubt the most charismatic figure I have ever seen. Even standing in the middle of a mud-soaked field some seventy yards from the stage his whole persona is spell binding.

"The set followed the pattern of the British

tour earlier in the year although the old Rainbow classic Stargazer was inserted as a treat for the fans. And towards the end of the night Cozy Powell played his last Rainbow drum solo which finished with fireworks filling the air.

"After that it hardly seemed possible for things to get wilder, but they did for after encores of 'All Night Long,' 'Will You Still Love Me Tomorrow,' and 'Long Live Rock 'n' Roll' Blackmore smashed his guitar and set fire to a dummy amplifier while fireworks filled the night sky. Perhaps now Donington will become a regular venue for rock festivals. If this happens then mud withstanding. it's great news for Tamworth music lovers."

****

Donington Park site manager Mike Goode said, "The concert went exactly as we had forecast and have no doubt that we will be welcomed back to do another one next year. It cost more than £500,000 to put on but indications are that we will make a profit."

Mrs Lillah Hooley, a member of Castle Donington Parish Council who strongly opposed the festival said: "My phone was ringing constantly with complaints from local people. We are not killjoys, but we really have had the brunt end of this event. People were going through our village until 1:00am leaving behind on the roads rubbish and cans and bottles. The noise level was high and

many could not sleep. We want to hold discussions to prevent a similar concert being held next year."

Stagehands worked through the night loading equipment on to forty articulated lorries and clearing the site for a motorcycle race the following day. Staff picked up tons of rubbish strewn across the centre of the circuit, but it wasn't until the Tuesday that the giant stage was taken down.

Talking to the *Hull Daily Mail*, eighteen-year-old Karen Walker said, "The festival was fantastic. We all got covered in mud—and some of us got caught in a mud fight—but it was all worthwhile to see bands like Rainbow and Scorpions. I would have paid £20 to go."

I Saw You Standing Down By The Stage

Alan Stutz—a long-time personal friend of the author—attended the gig. Alan has also kept day-to-day diaries since 1978 and his writings for 16th August 1980 mentioned, "The day started at 8:30 with some friends and I making our way to Castle Donington. We arrived at twelve and were confronted by a sea of mud, and a very expensive car park. Then followed standing in a chip queue for two hours, during which Touch, Riot and Saxon were on (nothing missed there!) April Wine were next who were average, then the Scorpions who were excellent. After Scorpions came Judas Priest, with a lot of hilarious over the top posing. They played a great set which was highly enjoyable. After that Rainbow came on after a long wait. When they played songs, they were very good, when they played solos they were crap. The fireworks brought a spectacular end to the day. Got home at 4:00 am, knackered."

In a *More Black than Purple* magazine article, reader Paul Raymond recalled his thoughts:

Donington was my first festival at the grand old age of seventeen — not being much of a Zeppelin fan I had given Knebworth a miss, and so Monsters of Rock was to be something of a new experience. Armed with a so-called 'two-man' tent, myself and one of my mates (more were to meet up at the Reading festival the following weekend) set off from deepest, darkest Bridport in Dorset to the Donington race circuit. The journey itself was uneventful and with the tent perfectly pitched by early evening it made sense to check out the surroundings, although as it turned out there was little to see. The only thing of interest (not sure exactly what the time would have been) was Rainbow's soundcheck on the Friday night— the closest to which I could get was stood behind an entrance gate, but at least I got to hear Ritchie live for the first time.

Having made it into the festival site the next morning, one of the first things that became apparent was the lack of facilities... to the extent that as the day unfolded it became easier and easier to miss a whole act just by queuing for a drink!

As far as the bands performed, the line-up was generally strong, from opening act Touch (I did notice the singer having difficulties at one point but back then I did not realise that he had in fact swallowed a bee!) it was all pretty good, although

apart from Judas Priest the only other band I was familiar with was Rainbow. I wasn't sure quite what to expect during that final wait as darkness set in, but when Rainbow finally took to the stage any concerns about not living up to expectations were immediately dismissed. From the intro to the finale I enjoyed the whole show, but for some bizarre reason the stand out track for me was the cover of Carole King's 'Will You Still Love Me Tomorrow'—there was just something about the silence that followed whatever the previous song was, coupled with the breeze, Ritchie then playing the opening chords, and then Graham Bonnet coming in with the vocals...

The concert finished with a very loud and visual firework display and then it was a return to silence and a wade through a sea of bottles, cartons and cans. That was my only visit to Donington, so quite brief memories of a Monsters of Rock festival—I just hope that one day someone will uncover the Rainbow film footage.

Paul Raymond

I was just in front of the PA tower, I took pictures between Riot and April Wine on a trip to the burger van queue. After Priest finished a lot of people left so I managed to get right down to the barrier.

Ken Williams

I remember it well. Riot had just started as we were entering. Happy days.
Ian White

The start of my festival addiction. Loved the Monsters of Rock.
Tina Smith

The first one! The original Monsters of Rock. Initially it was planned as a one-off event, just a big way for Rainbow to end their *Down To Earth* tour. It quickly shaped up into something much bigger.

I'd been to see Led Zeppelin at Knebworth the previous year, which had been my first festival. It made a big impression on me and resulted in me going to at least one major festival every year for the next two decades.

The Monsters of Rock show was less eclectic than previous festivals, specialising instead on the recent interest in Heavy Metal, in particular, the New Wave Of British Heavy Metal that a lot of older bands like Rainbow and, second on the bill, Judas Priest were riding high. Saxon were the NWOBHM representatives here with Scorpions from Germany, April Wine from Canada and American bands Riot & Touch completing the bill.

The host for the day was DJ Neal Kaye who I'd seen touring with Iron Maiden earlier in the year. He was great and really kept the momentum up in between acts.

I lived in Stockport, Cheshire at the time and had decided to catch one of the charted coaches with my (then) girlfriend Debbie, which bizarrely left at midnight on the Friday from the centre of Manchester. It's only a seventy-mile journey so we arrived way too early and ended up 'hanging around' outside the gate for hours drinking beer for breakfast. My brother had taken the more sensible option of biking there with his friend Paul, who was more commonly known as Thermos.

The site was well organised in terms of admission and car parking, well it should've been really as an already established sporting venue. The main difference was the total camping ban, even then it still didn't deter everyone and quite a few tents began to pop up in the surrounding fields.

Inside the arena there were plenty of eateries and toilets but no bars. But that was okay, 'cos you could take you own booze in. I seem to remember the weather being pretty good that day too.

The bands performances and events have been well documented over the years, the lead singer of Touch swallowing a bee for example. I don't remember too much about Touch or Riot, second band on. It was Saxon that caught my attention first; they'd already had a couple of hits so were really the first 'name' band on the bill. They warmed the crowd up well with a ten-song set that included their two hits of that year 'Wheels Of

Steel' and '747 (Strangers In The Night)'.

Next up were April Wine who I found a little boring, the exception being their rip-roaring rendition of King Crimson's '21st Century Schizoid Man.' The Scorpions received the biggest cheer (so far) as they walked onstage. They were arguably the first band up that people had actually come to see having proved themselves to be an exciting live act. They were in the perfect place at the perfect time and played a blinder.

Judas Priest had been around for ages; even back in 1980 they were considered part of the 'old school.' Their latest album *British Steel* had given them a new lease of life and won a new audience in the NWOBHM fan base. They couldn't fail, especially when Rob Halford arrived onstage riding a Harley. It was during this set when Halford hinted that this was to become an annual event... how right he was.

As for Rainbow, well, no surprises really. I'd already seen them earlier on the tour up in Manchester and this show was very similar. A few more pyrotechnics, an over the top drum solo (Cozy's last with the band but not his last at Donington) an equally over the top guitar smashing routine and some extremely over the top fireworks at the end... oh, and they added 'Stargazer' to the set, easily their best song.

All in all, the first Donington festival was pretty bloody good and still stands high on my list. Due to the shape of the site everyone got a good view

and there was the additional advantage of a big screen. The trip back on the coach was no picnic though... never again!
Ashley Haynes

Such a fantastic line up for my first outdoors rock event ever. I have a pirate DVD copy of the Rainbow set from that day. Looking back it really was a good show and I am pleased to relive it through the DVD occasionally. I still have my official Monsters of Rock T-shirt which is still unworn but alas it seems to have shrunk in the drawer! Any chance of the BBC screening the Rainbow footage from the day? A great day full of great memories.
Mike Harrold

My first ever festival... and still without doubt, the best.
Glen Pimborough

I don't think it rained but it had as I do recall mud. Rainbow were sublime, Ritchie was in awesome form especially on 'Stargazer'. April Wine were there as well, and I remember one side of my face was sunburnt quite badly. I also seem to recall bottles of Newcastle Brown that had to be left in the car.
Simon Richards

I am probably fortunate that I was at the right age at the time of the first festival (17 years old) to be able to go on to attend all the festivals. In fact (although a little sad in hindsight) during the eighties it was my highlight of the year each year.

I would organise the tickets, the transport (five of us in a Ford Cortina in 1980 to twenty of us in two transit vans in '87 and '88), the banners & flagpoles (these became more ambitious every time with flags and flashing lights etc being added each year, some people actually used our flagpoles as meeting points), and of course... the beer. Over the years the rules for which containers you could use for carrying your beer in changed from using virtually whatever you liked to not being able to use anything at all, but the daftest idea was probably when you could use a 2-litre bottle as long as the top and neck had been cut off, this made it almost impossible to carry when full.

Most people would probably say that spending all day in a (mostly muddy—Donington was famed for its mud way before Glastonbury) field with up to 100 thousand denim and leather clad rockers listening to a sometimes inaudible racket was their version of Hell, but to me it has given me some of the greatest memories of my life and I am proud to claim that I attended them all and loved every minute of it.

In 1980 I had never attended an outdoor festival before, so my excitement was at fever pitch during the preceding week, especially as my all-time hero (still is to this day) Ritchie Blackmore would be headlining. There were all sorts of rumours about Blackmore playing a major solo on top of the speaker stacks way above the stage (as it happened this didn't take place due to some mechanical lift failure apparently).

My very first view of Donington (and my earliest memory) was as we approached the entrances from the car park, I could see the merchandise stalls from afar with the Rainbow *Down To Earth* knitted scarves pinned to the top of the marquees. I had missed out on one of these scarves from the tour earlier in the year, so my wallet was honed into buying one as soon as we got in. I still have it today (along with all the festival t-shirts and programmes from every year).

I also recall that there was a Greenpeace stall, selling 'what else' but 'Rainbow Warrior' t-shirts. There was also an official Rainbow fan club stall on site.

Musically the highlight of the day (and probably of any day) was the way Rainbow segued 'Since You Been Gone' into 'Somewhere Over The Rainbow' and then straight into 'Stargazer' (my favourite song ever)... even though Graham Bonnet did mess the words up a bit. Cozy Powell's '1812 Overture' drum solo went off with its usual bang and Blackmore's (stage managed) setting fire to a speaker stack during his guitar onslaught finale were other fond memories of the headlining act.

I remember getting into a queue for a burger approximately twenty minutes prior to Judas Priests' set and still being stood in the same place in the queue some one and a half hours later after they had left the stage. I think the stallholder must have been a Priest fan.

To me the Scorpions were playing as well as they ever did at that time in their career (prior to the MTV-friendly version we got a few years later) and their set was as faultless as ever (I saw them three times during 1980). I recall 'Pictured Life' being a particular favourite of mine at the time.

Saxon were also on a roll on the back of their nationwide *Wheels Of Steel* tour. They went down very well.

Of the other bands I can only really remember April Wine being okay. The weather on the day was fine, but the preceding fortnight continuous rain had made the site a mud bath. The toilets were appalling!
Paul Hartshorn

A really great line-up. I do not remember it raining—that was 1981. Rainbow, Judas Priest and the Scorpions were excellent. Especially as Rainbow did 'Stargazer' for the first time since their first tour. I also remember a BBC *Rock Week* special shown on BBC2 which featured about forty minutes of Rainbow. What are the chances of releasing the whole concert?
Paul Addison

We drove through the night from Edinburgh, set up a tent and opened a can of beer at 8:00am. That's what you do at seventeen, right? It was a great event, but I was new to festivals and didn't really enjoy the piss filled bottles flying about the place.
Kenny Stewart

A great gig: my first festival. What a way to start. DJ announcing at 16:00, "Could (forget kids name) please go to the main gate, as his mum has come to take him home." 50,000 people sit down en masse.
Ian Butler

Brilliant, went down with a mate (Jamie A Moore) on one of the Glasgow Apollo buses). Totally under prepared, £8.50 to get in on the day. Amazing day. Still have the ticket attached to the compilation album that was brought out. Only one of the video screens worked. But I saw Rainbow for the first time. And a German band Scorpions were bloody ace! Best money ever spent on a gig!
Alan Thomson

Cycled there. Took me an hour to find my bike afterwards in the car park. It was a long 15 miles home, but worth it! Only downer: a band like Rainbow playing 'Will You Still Love Me Tomorrow'!
Chris Lee

Great line-up of bands, mushy Peas and April Wine: What a day.
David Whitfield

My first outdoor festival, brilliant!
Pete Watson

My first concert, some of us from school went.
Andy Francis

I was just in front of the PA tower. What a great gig!
Robert Sas

Appendices

Set lists

Touch: *My Life Depends On You / Last Chance For Love / Don't You Know What Love Is / Black Star / So High / When The Spirit Moves You / Yes (You Need To Rock 'n' Roll) / Listen (Can You Feel It) //*

Riot: *Warrior / Overdrive / Rock City / Back on the Non-Stop / Kick Down the Wall / Train Kept A-Rollin' / Road Racin' //*

Saxon: *Motorcycle Man / Still Fit to Boogie / Freeway Mad / Backs to the Wall / Wheels of Steel / Bap Shoo Ap / 747 (Strangers in the Night) / Stallions of the Highway / Machine Gun //*

April Wine: *Oowatanite / Get Ready For Love / I Like To Rock / Ladies Man / Before The Dawn / 21st Century Schizoid Man / Roller / Don't Push Me Around //*

Scorpions: *Lovedrive / Don't Make No Promises (Your Body Can't Keep) / Loving You Sunday Morning / We'll Burn the Sky / The Zoo / Always Somewhere / Pictured Life / Robot Man / Another Piece of Meat / Can't Get Enough //*

Judas Priest: *Hell Bent For Leather / The Ripper / Running Wild / Living After Midnight / Sinner / Beyond the Realms of Death / You Don't Have to Be Old to Be Wise / Grinder / Victim of Changes / The Green Manalishi (With the Two Prong Crown) / Tyrant //*

Rainbow: *Intro: Land Of Hope & Glory intro to Countdown-Over The Rainbow / Eyes Of The World / Love's No Friend / Greensleeves / Since You Been Gone / Over The Rainbow-Stargazer / Man On The Silver Mountain / Catch The Rainbow / Keyboard intro to Lost In Hollywood / guitar solo (feat. Light In The Black-Ode To Joy) / Keyboard solo / Drum solo / Lost in Hollywood reprise / Lazy-All Night Long-Blues / Will You Love Me Tomorrow / Long Live Rock 'n' Roll-Kill The King-Long Live Rock 'n' Roll / Over The Rainbow //*

Recordings

A souvenir single vinyl album—unsurprisingly called *Monsters Of Rock*—was released by Polydor on 10th October.

It featured performances from all the acts except Judas Priest, who had opted out on the strength that they didn't want any other recordings to conflict with their own live album *Unleashed In The East*.

The track listing is as follows:

Side 1

Rainbow–   Stargazer (8:21)

Scorpions– Loving You Sunday Morning (4:58)

Scorpions– Another Piece Of Meat (4:43)

Saxon– Backs To The Wall (3:29)

Side 2

Rainbow–All Night Long (7:58)

April Wine– I Like To Rock (3:58)

Touch– Don't Ya Know What Love Is? (3:55)

Riot– Road Racin' (7:23)

It achieved a creditable No.16 in the UK album charts.

The cassette version included bonus tracks 'The Zoo' by Scorpions and Saxon's 'Freeway Mad.'

The US version had a different sleeve with aerial shots of the gig on the front cover and on the back cover a British "Bobbie" overseeing the traffic controls that were in place.

Saxon's forty-minute set was released some years later as a live CD on the Angel Air label.

Rainbow's set was also filmed and twenty-nine minutes of it was brutally edited into "highlights" and aired on BBC2 as part of *Rock Week* on Thursday 9th October.

The edit was made by the BBC although the footage was produced by Green Back Films, formed in the 1970s by Aubrey Powell, Storm Thorgerson and Peter Christopherson as an offshoot of their design company Hipgnosis.

The audio was recorded by the Manor Mobile, a mobile recording studio owned by Richard Branson. Despite extensive searches ever since the complete film footage of Rainbow's 104-minute show has not yet been located.

Although he has since passed away, the film's director Nigel Lesmoir-Gordon told the author that he had no recollection as to what happened to the rushes after sending them to the BBC for editing.

The story of the first Monsters Of Rock

RECORD REVIEW

'Monsters of Rock' ✲✲

It came as a surprise to me when this year's heavy metal dominated Reading Festival sold out well in advance. I hadn't realised that the headbangers had returned in such force. Unfortunately for HM fans, there is no permanent record of the Reading bash available. However, the 'Monsters of Rock' album is a momento of last summer's other HM gathering and, in my opinion, the bill at Donnington was better than any single day at Reading........ but, each to his own.

Rainbow, the headlining act, pop up with 'All night long' and 'Stargazer' in their last appearance with Cozy Powell on the skins (the drum kind, boys). The other contributors are The Scorpions, Saxon, April Wine, Touch and Riot. It's a nice souvenir for those who were there and if you weren't there you're probably not interested in heavy metal and may as well forget you read the last two paragraphs.

✲✲✲✲✲ Essential Listening
✲✲✲✲ Excellent
✲✲✲ Good
✲✲ Fair
✲ Poor

Steve Henderson

Discography

Monsters Of Rock
Polydor, 2488 810, UK 1980

Castle Donnington:
Monsters Of Rock
Polydor, PD-1-6311, USA 1980

Saxon - Live At Donnington 1980
Angel Air Records, SJPCD045, UK 1996
Tracks: Motorcycle Man / Still Fit To Boogie / Freeway Mad / Backs To The Wall / Wheels Of Steel / Bap Shoo Ap / 747 (Strangers In The Night) / Stallions Of The Highway / Machine Gun //

All above releases misspell Donington as Donnington.

**Rainbow –
Monsters Of Rock:
Live At Donington 1980**
Eagle Vision, EAGDV056,
UK, 22nd April 2016

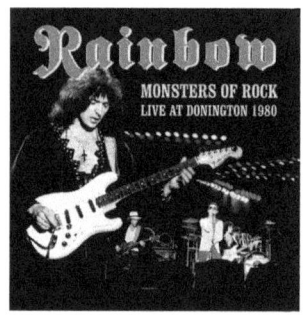

DVD: Lazy / All Night Long / Catch The Rainbow / Eyes Of The World / Ritchie Blackmore Guitar Solo / Difficult To Cure / Will You Love Me Tomorrow / Long Live Rock 'N' Roll //

CD: Band Warm-Up - Over The Rainbow - Eyes Of The World / Since You Been Gone / Over The Rainbow (Reprise) / Stargazer / Catch The Rainbow / Nutcracker (Keyboard Solo) - Toccata & Fugue In D Minor (Keyboard Solo) / Lost In Hollywood, Guitar Solo / Difficult To Cure (Beethoven's Ninth) Keyboard Solo / Smoke On The Water (Keyboard Solo) / Sailor's Hornpipe (Keyboard Solo)   / Drum Solo, 1812 Overture (Drum Solo) / Lost In Hollywood (Reprise) / Lazy / All Night Long / Blues / Will You Love Me Tomorrow / Long Live Rock 'n' Roll //

Released as a double disc, it includes a DVD of the 29-minute BBC video edit. The audio is incomplete as they wanted to keep it to a single disc. However, the full audio was released as a double CD in Japan (Ward Records, GQCS-90141~3)

Acknowledgements

Rev Barker at www.ukrockfestivals.com, Roy Davies, Rene Nethitt, Graham Oliver, Peter Purnell at Angel Air Music, the late Paul Raymond, Laura Shenton, Alan Stutz, Drew Thompson at Thompson Music Management.

Thanks to all the fans who contributed recollections.

Rainbow

Tickets £7.50 adv. £8.50 on the day
SAT 16th AUG First Band 1.00pm
DONNINGTON PARK (NR. DERBY)
Gates Open 9.00am

Nº 99696

The story of the first Monsters Of Rock

Knocking the rock — and repeats

I don't know that they'll be all that many who would say quite the same about tonight's Rock Week (BBC2) features. First off we're whisked back to the days of Van Morrison At The Rainbow which made television history as the first simultaneous rock programme on stereo radio and The Old Grey Whistle Test. The Caledonia Soul Orchestra make with the noise there, while later the head-banging, heavy metal brigade blast your eardrums with more than just colour as Rainbow play a gig at Castle Donington. These are clips from the Monsters of Rock concert, concentrating largely on Cozy Powell and Rainbow. You'll need very catholic tastes in music and, might I suggest, earplugs to appreciate it to the full.

By Melvyn Briggs

Other titles from Wymer Publishing that might interest you:

A Hart Life
978-1-908724-04-5
Colin Hart with Dick Allix

Swords & Tequilla: Riot's Classic First Decade
978-1-912782-15-4
Martin Popoff

Smokin' Valves:
A Headbanger's Guide to 900 NWOBHM Records
978-1-912782-10-9
Martin Popoff

Wheels Of Steel:
The Explosive Early Years of NWOBHM
978-1-912782-18-5
Martin Popoff

This Means War:
The Sunset Years of NWOBHM
978-1-912782-23-9
Martin Popoff

Sensitive To Light:
The Rainbow Story
978-1-912782-40-6
Martin Popoff

Denim And Leather:
Saxon's First Ten Years
978-1-912782-64-2
Martin Popoff

Judas Priest:
Decade Of Domination
978-1-912782-63-5
Martin Popoff

Judas Priest:
Turbo 'til Now
978-1-912782-73-4
Martin Popoff

Rainbow Straight Between The Eyes:
In-depth
978-1-912782-96-3
Laura Shenton

Ritchie Blackmore A Life In Vision
978-1-915246-30-1
Jerry Bloom

Run With The Wolf:
Rainbow On Record
978-1-915246-64-6
Martin Popoff

Dance With The Devil:
The Cozy Powell Story - Revised & Expanded
978-1-915246-65-3
Laura Shenton

Cozy Powell A Life In Vision
978-1-915246-66-0
Laura Shenton

Taken by Force:
Sixty Years of Scorpions
978-1-915246-88-2
Martin Popoff

When Evening Falls:
Rainbow 1974-77
978-1-915246-92-9
Roy Davies

Searching In The Darkness:
Rainbow 1978-81
978-1-915246-93-6
Roy Davies

Lost In A Distant Dream:
Rainbow 1982-84, 1994-97, 2016-19
978-1-915246-94-3
Roy Davies

www.ingramcontent.com/pod-product-compliance
Lightning Source LLC
Chambersburg PA
CBHW042136160426
43200CB00019B/2949